# Eternity by the Stars

Louis-Auguste Blanqui

# Eternity by the Stars

## An Astronomical Hypothesis

Translated and with an Introduction
by Frank Chouraqui

ERIS

**ERIS**

265 Riverside Drive
New York, NY 10025



First published in 2013 by Contra Mundum Press

ISBN 978-1-971559-35-3

# Contents

*To Keith Ansell-Pearson*

# At the Crossroads of History

## Blanqui at the Castle of the Bull

# I

The Fort du Taureau (or Castle of the Bull) is an ellipse-shaped fortified island lying half-a-mile outside of the rocky shores of Morlaix at a place where, after briefly morphing into the English Channel, the Atlantic Ocean finally returns in the guise of the North Sea. It is also the place where, in keeping with the dubious honor made by weak regimes to figures whose ideas are more dangerous than their bodies, the fragile "Executive Power" of Adolphe Thiers—a transitional government squeezed between Napoleon III's Second Empire and the Third Republic—decided to wall up its most famous revolutionary, in the hope that isolation would let his power dwindle and his existence fade away into nothingness. Standing on the other side of the bargain, Louis-Auguste Blanqui was left no choice but to wager, on the contrary, that survival always contained the possibility of return. The post-revolutionary refusal of the absolute is nowhere so well illustrated as in these concrete blocks scattered across the sea, monuments to the messy arrangements between fearful regimes that compromise their future for the sake of their present and their visionary dissidents, who accept the opposing end of the bargain, for revolution in all its incarnations is always a projection towards the future. It is there, as the sole inmate of a sea prison, deprived of vision by guards instructed to shoot him if he approached the window, that Blanqui conceived *Eternity by the Stars*. A strange book by any count, *Eternity by the Stars* is also the expression of a strange movement in the soul of its author. Coming from a man of action, practical in the extreme, who didn't know any courage other than physical, and any human virtue other than courage, Blanqui's confinement could only mean the beginning of an unheard-of form of thinking. The values are of course still there, deliberately simplistic and brutally well-defined, so as to never infringe on the potential for action: the future must be forced into the present, freedom is always the freedom to act, and the possible can never be reduced to the real; the tone and the project however, are now as different as can be.

At the Castle of the Bull, Blanqui found himself surrounded by a world of repetition. In a circular cell with a vaulted ceiling, listening to the ebb and flow of the sea, and the repetitive beating of the waves, Blanqui offers us a reflection on missed opportunities and the crossroads of history. *Eternity by the Stars* puts forward the major thesis that all is possible and that all that is possible is actual. The perceived difference between actual and possible is only a topological difference, the only limitation of man is the limitation of his senses, for worlds are only differentiated by the realm of the sensations of every given person. By establishing the coexistence of all events, Blanqui once again places the human mind at the core of the fate of the universe, for *Eternity by the Stars* replaces the disjunctive logic of linear time with a conjunctive logic in which understanding blends into imagination, and the human mind merges into a cosmic reality where the possible is simply a name of the actual, finally collapsing the unfolding of time into an unfolded space. From the confinement of his cell, Blanqui gave flesh in an unheard-of manner to the commonplace intuition he shared with all the wretches in past, present, or future jails: the freedom to think and the freedom to write is as real as any freedom. If the possible is really the conceivable and imaginings can be written down, words on the page signify not the musings of their author, but the map of the universe itself as Blanqui ceaselessly crosses the conventional separation of text and reality. For in *Eterni-ty*, it is "globes pouring out of the quill by the billions" that we witness, and it is the time of naming worlds that measures the time of interstellar travel: under his astronomer's cloak, Blanqui the Promethean atheist, remains, and his verdict is that human understanding is in fact the understanding of a god, an understanding that *conceives* worlds in the strong sense of the word, and his telling the world is the same as the world it tells. In eternity, man and god are the same, for the human's access to the world constitutes it in ways heretofore reserved to divinities. At the Castle of the Bull, reduced to his potential, a man of action could only be left to his own musings on the falsity of the difference between potential and action.

The arrest of Blanqui on March 17, 1871, and his subsequent confinement at the Bull, were far from being his first imprisonment. In fact, if we include the sentence delivered to him later, on February 15, 1872, Blanqui had been sentenced to prison more than nine times between 1831 and 1872, including, in addition to minor penalties, two death sentences, two life sentences, one exile sentence and two sentences of 10 and 4 years respectively. As for most political prisoners in nineteenth–century France, the application of such sentences was chaotic, interrupted and commuted by the fancy of complex and capricious political games.

Born in 1814 to a bourgeois family, Blanqui's life offers a summary of the vicissitudes of the socially-event-ful $19^{th}$ century. For Blanqui was the man of every battle; indeed, the inventor-discoverer of political battlefields: if the war is between the rich and the poor, as most of the socialist left contended, this means that any power given by the bourgeoisie to the proletariat must be viewed with suspicion; indeed, it must be viewed as a sign that the proletariat must take stock of its own power: for every concession of the bourgeoisie is only a faint reflection of the power of a proletariat suffering from a chronic inability to recognize its own power. The state offers elections? They should be banned. The state offers social reform? We demand revolution. The state offers social mobility? This no longer concerns bourgeoisie and proletariat, but humans, and the struggle should be personalized.

Blanqui's political genius was constantly busy assessing the political systems that succeeded each other, locating their weaknesses like a general on the battlefield, before tying the strategic flaws of the enemy to an ideological and moral failing: not only can power be taken on; it must, on moral grounds, be taken down. The duty of opposition is not only determined by the iniquity of those in power, it is also in and of itself the natural place of the honest man. In a word: power coincides with depravation, and institutions are inhuman.

It was the last throes of a typically French experiment in constitutional monarchy that gave Blanqui a first taste of the weakness of all regimes, as well as a first experience of missed opportunity. In 1839, he was one of the leaders of a narrowly defeated Parisian insurrection against Louis-Philippe's July Monarchy. The first death sentence ensued. The rule of Louis-Philippe would indeed survive widespread unrest until the famous revolution of 1848. A success by all counts, that uprising ushered the return of the Republic, that is to say, nothing more than the arrival of a new enemy in the eyes of Blanqui's radicalism. He would walk out of his cell ten years later, with the Republic long gone, to see an emperor where a king had been ousted. This led to four years of prison and an escape, followed by a string of failed uprisings leading up to the famous Paris Commune (March–May 1871). Of course, by the time the Commune had been established and crushed by Thiers, Blanqui was already held captive again: a missed opportunity for history and a most cruel exclusion from the only three months of the 19th century when the Paris air was worth anything to Blanqui's political lungs. It is hardly any wonder that after four narrowly failed revolutions, countless foiled conspiracies and prison cells, Blanqui's mind began turning to a deeply speculative reflection on missed opportunities.

## II

*Eternity by the Stars* was written at the Fort du Taureau, between the end of May and the middle of November 1871, and published on February 20, 1872, three days after Blanqui was sentenced to life imprisonment by a Versailles tribunal. However, the manuscript was part of Blanqui's plans for his legal defense, and he insists in a letter to his sister of January 31, 1872, that it be published ahead of his trial, distributed to the press and to the members of the Assembly, and left in plain sight within the Tribunal chambers at Versailles. On May 28, 1872, still hopeful for a revision of his trial, he requests that his correspondent give copies of *Eternity by the Stars* to assemblymen Edmond Adam and Jules Barthélémy-Saint-Hilaire, two close allies of Thiers', with instruction to "remind both men that my case is not in the hands of the committee of the stars [*la commission des astres*], but of Thiers alone."[1] Was Blanqui intentionally renaming the pardons committee [*la commission des grâces*], in which he placed all his hopes, by changing its name to "the committee of the stars" [*la commission des astres*]? In their insightful and impassioned presentation of their French edition of *Eternity by the Stars*, Miguel Abensour and Valentin Pelosse, who quote this letter without commenting on this odd phrasing, go to great lengths to refute the alleged misconception that the pamphlet was an expression of *ressentiment*, that is to say, an appeal to the abstract intended to offset the material frustration of imprisonment and political oppression, perhaps even endowed a prophetic warning aimed at the tyrant from a recluse with the ability to read the stars. A man like Blanqui, a French socialist of the post-Enlightenment breed, had always recognized only one judge and one tribunal, for himself and his fellowmen, and this judge was nature conceived as a benevolent, moral guarantor of human rights.[2] Linguistic slip or not, ascetic or not, *Eternity by the Stars* is nothing else than a secular plea to the gods of science, the desperate plea of the wretched of the earth for being allowed into a whole in which defeat is never final, mistakes can be redeemed, missed opportunities recur, and where the crossroads of history leave no road untraveled. The stars are indeed Blanqui's only pardons committee.

The main claim of *Eternity by the Stars* is that the discrepancy between a limited—albeit great—number of possible events and the infinity of time and space necessitates the infinite repetition of all possible events.

This "hypothesis" is supported by four key theses: firstly, that space is material and infinite, and therefore, that matter itself is infinite (chapters I and II). Secondly, that all matter is the result of a chemical organization of a limited number of elements. Blanqui uses spectral analysis to suggest that the number of chemical elements present across the universe is limited. He recognizes that new ones may be discovered in the future beyond the 64 already identified in his time, and assumes that the number might eventually reach 100 (chapter IV). Thirdly, all such matter can only be organized into solar systems, for the only rules applying to all matter are the rules of Newton's celestial mechanics as developed by Laplace (chapters V and VI). This means that phenomena that seem to escape such rules, like comets, are either immaterial or simply misunderstood, and in any case, do not present a threat to Blanqui's argument (chapter V). Finally, Blanqui addresses the difficult question of origins, which he accused Laplace of "dodging." Unlike Laplace, Blanqui places the infinite at the center of his argument, and is therefore compelled to tackle it directly. He does so by making the infinite prevail over the need for origins: worlds constantly become resurrected and reincarnated, as only a limited amount of matter is ever available in the world, and what makes a world is simply a certain organization of such matter, and its death is but an undoing of this organization, that is to say, only a transformation into another organization, into another world (chapter VI). In addition to these explicit arguments, we should stress two crucial assumptions apparently taken for granted by Blanqui. The first is his atomism, which makes him repeatedly state that "matter cannot diminish or increase by one atom," for it is only the combination of a limited (atomistic) intensive space and an unlimited extensive space that can lead to Blanqui's statistical speculation. Secondly, matter thus conceived must be stable in amount; that is to say, every possible event must be accounted for as a reorganization of a given amount of matter and not a creation in any radical sense of the word. Although supported by the core of Lavoisier's chemistry and his famous affirmation of the law of conservation of mass in 1789, often difficult to distinguish from the now disproven thesis of conservation of matter, it is however these very assumptions that would cause Blanqui's thesis to perish at the hands of quantum physics, and its groundbreaking exploitation of the distinction between mass and matter.[3]

These four theses and two assumptions constitute the groundwork for Blanqui's thesis and in the first page of chapter VII, he considers the job complete. He concludes:

> Nothing but stellar systems can be built, and a hundred *simple bodies* are the sole materials; this is a lot of labor and few tools. Admittedly, with such a monotonous plan and such a small variety of elements, it is difficult to engender enough different combinations to populate the infinite. Resorting to repetitions becomes necessary.

This in turn implies that every possible event is in fact actual too, and repeated infinitely through time (they will recur infinitely) and space (an infinite number of fully identical events are taking place at the same time throughout the cosmos).

All of Blanqui's hypotheses can be brought back to relatively few scientific readings on his part. In fact, there is no definite evidence that Blanqui read more than two or three books, all of them regarded by their own authors as works of vulgarization: Pierre-Simon Laplace's *Exposition du système du monde* (1796) and Francois Arago's *Astronomie populaire* (1855), and perhaps his *Des comètes en général* (1832).

## III

On several levels, Blanqui's relationship with both Laplace and Arago is ambiguous. Although he is his principal source, and his direct interlocutor, Laplace is also the most chastised of Blanqui's sources. Blanqui's very first mention of the great mathematician is also a declaration of defiance. He writes: "Laplace took his system from Herschel who took it from his telescope." One may be permitted to regard this formula an example of Blanqui's legendary rhetoric of ambiguity: Herschel is summoned as an empirical caution ensuring that Blanqui's own speculations—based on Laplace's—remain grounded in observation. But by a subtle sleight of hand, this legitimacy seems to do no good to Laplace himself, who is left looking like a vulgar plagiarist. In fact, much of Blanqui's relationship with science surfaces here: observations must be scientific, but systematic elaborations must be left to men of action and of imagination. Any figure who, like Laplace, intends to remain within the confines of the sciences while dabbling in systematic thought will become only a parody of a scientist, and a parody of a politician. Further, it could be said that Blanqui, in his ambiguous relationship with Laplace, announces in fact one of the key dimensions of his hypothesis, that of a politics of science. In a century replete with great men of science who were also great public servants (Laplace himself, Arago, Raspail, among many others), Blanqui, in typically materialist fashion, is concerned with the implicit connection between the disinterested desire for knowledge and the need to respond to the constant call for action, that he calls poverty, exclusion, and oppression. It is, in fact, Blanqui's unabashed impatience with political arguments and demonstrations in favor of (often rash) action that alienated many of his radical colleagues. As regards Laplace, Blanqui's complaint is double: Firstly, Laplace was the kind of man that any good socialist should stay away from, and so, for political reasons. Secondly, Laplace was unable to go far enough in his systematic forays, precisely because of his reprehensible taste for scientific caution, or in Blanqui's terms, his obsession with mathematics and his defiance toward empirical observation (in this sense, Herschel remains unaffected by Blanqui's attacks). Of course, to Blanqui's mind, the two criticisms—one *ad hominem* based on Laplace's politics and the other based on his scientific work—are related. For the distinction of a man from his work is but a bourgeois myth designed to maintain the paramount myth of interiority, a myth whose political efficiency is everywhere verified and deplorable. The implication, of course, is that without Blanqui, Laplace's system would never have crossed the Rubicon that separates science from matters of ethics, metaphysics, and politics.

Let us return to Blanqui's complaint that Laplace "dodged" the question of origins, for here again, the political criticism is used to fuel a scientific attack. The "dodging" Blanqui alludes to is Laplace's famous yet romanticized response to Napoleon's surprise at seeing no mention of God or of his Creation in Laplace's *Exposition*. Laplace is said to have responded in terms that epitomize the entire scientific project: "But Sire, I had no need of that hypothesis." Such a response could only please Blanqui, a staunch secularist himself, but he also laments that it falls short of a formal rejection of God. If Laplace's hypothesis, namely that the solar system comes from a concentrated nebula, was insufficient, it is because by making its object the solar system as we know it now, it leaves the *before* and the *outside* of the universe open to extravagant "hypotheses," maintaining gaps for the entirety of the divine to pour into. Blanqui's project, on the contrary, is to propose a cosmology that precludes any outside by placing the concept of the infinite at its core.

It doesn't matter to Blanqui, it seems, that Laplace himself wrote a seminal work of philosophy with his *Essai philosophique sur les probabilités*, which concludes with these words:

> To anyone who would consider that even with regard to the very things that cannot be submitted to calculations, [the science of probabilities] offers the most assured insights susceptible to guide us in our judgments, and the fact that it teaches one to refrain from illusions that often lead us astray, it shall become clear that there is no science more worthy of our meditations, and which would be introduced into our public instruction system more profitably.[4]

This could not fail to remind us of Blanqui's own unpub-lished "Essai sur l'enseignement de la cosmographie," written in the very months of the Castle of the Bull, where the teaching of cosmography based on a deterministic use of probabilities is presented as an antidote to all superstitions and religions and therefore should, to Blanqui's (and Laplace's) mind, be included in all school curricula.

By any count, Laplace came very close to Blanqui's cosmological conclusions. And measuring Blanqui's "astronomical hypothesis" against the scientific genius of Laplace is nothing short of vain. The point is not that Laplace showed no interest in politics—he did, actively—but that he saw a distinction between politics and science and, according to Blanqui, this distinction is itself political, that is, bourgeois and conservative.

Was Blanqui's judgment of Laplace unfair? Certain-ly, but is it fair for us to expect from Blanqui that he judge a mathematician in scientific terms? Blanqui's complaint, although wrapped in the pretense of science, is not scientific; it has to do with a politics of science, and seen from this angle, it makes sense. The mathematician Jean-Pierre Kahane is correct, it seems, when he points out how in his *Philosophical Essay* Laplace limited himself to finite models to talk both about the finite *and* the infinite. He is also correct when, in Laplace's defense, he notes: "this is no logical failure: for [Laplace], limit laws are but analytic tools designed to approach the proba- bilities involved in a finite model."[5] Approaching the finite by way of the infinite is good science indeed, but Blanqui complains, it is *only* science. On the contrary, as Blanqui's title should make plain, *Eternity by the Stars* proposes the opposite challenge: the infinite must be approached by way of the finite stellar observations we have in our possession. Once again, the apparently minor differences between Blanqui and his chosen opponent now appear as a full-fledged mutual exclusion: of the finite from the infinite, or of the infinite from the finite.

Laplace remained a scientist, and as a scientist, he remained wary of staking his entire system on the concept of the infinite, a concept that collapses his beloved separation of physics and metaphysics. Laplace, a wretched mathematician in Blanqui's eyes, was also a wretched servant of Napoleon. Whether factually true or not, there is no doubt that the anecdote relative to Laplace's exchange with Napoleon recalled above reflected Laplace's attitude fairly closely. Indeed, it was nothing but the response of the scientific spirit to the political animal. God and the infinite are speculations, hypotheses that scientists must do away with. If politics is the science of the possible, it is no science at all, and the political mind must be kept away from empirical science. No two men can be more opposed to each other than the totalitarian Emperor and the constant revolutionary, but they were both aware that science was nothing if not used for action, and that ideas came to life only through inspirations. If the duty of a good scientist is to remain within the bounds of physics, the role of the public figure is to break this separation: it is the spilling of knowledge into human emotion, morals, and myth that makes inspiration, and politicians win by inspiring.

This is the thinker's contribution: along with the difference between physics and metaphysics dear to Laplace, a concept like the infinite is able to collapse the difference between here and there, past and present, self and other, cosmology and metaphysics, metaphysics and ontology, possibility and actuality, and further, theory and practice. We must regard the lesson of Blanqui's speculation as the collapsing of difference in general for, as he writes: "as a whole as well as in detail, the universe is forever transformation and immanence." To him, the infinite signifies the final rejection of externality into nothingness, for any outside is an outside of the whole, that is, just like the comets he dismisses at length, a "nihility."

From within the infinite, Blanqui sees a purely democratic world surging forth, an extrapolation of his dear human brotherhood and solidarity, where not only men of a class, but all men become brothers; where not only mankind, but all objects become brothers. Comets are "homeless gypsies" the universal proletarians dispossessed of matter and thus condemned to be aimlessly roaming the vast expanses, like the wretched of the earth, stripped of material possessions, are left wandering in a world that cannot accept them as full citizens. Universes are "brother-worlds" unified only on the plane of immanence secured by Blanqui's infinite calculus, a calculus that strips any star of its alleged monarchic position in the closed world that precedes the establishment of the infinite. If suns are "kings" and solar systems "kingdoms," their authority collapses in the infinite, and the "kings" soon become nurturing "queens" stripped of authority and yet endowed with all duties to their kingdoms, true anarchic rulers, true public servants in fact, models for men of power everywhere, models that no one follows:

> The queens govern unknowingly their kingdoms by bestowing benefits to it. They do the sowing, but not the harvesting. They have the charges, but not the benefits. Although they are masters of force, they use it only for the sake of weakness... Dear stars! You shall find few imitators.

In this new, hallucinatory vision sprouting from within the narrow confines of a sea fortress, where any difference is only internal, where all is but a version of the other, where being oneself means being what one could have been and where being other means the same, Blanqui finds that his longing was always satisfied in reality, and that one's only task is to come to terms with the vanity of all myths of progress, for the longed-for brotherhood is always already there, a brotherhood of worlds, where oppressive regimes live alongside anarchic, socialist, and brotherly societies in harmony; a world where progress is not a task, but the name of another place, a world where existence is a man's and a galaxy's only justification, a world that has room for everything. Here is Blanqui's lesson to Laplace: the true infinite collapses the opposition of science and action, of theory and practice, and opens up, indeed, necessitates, a politics of science.

Blanqui's defiance toward scientific authorities, which borders on bad faith, is visible in his dealings with Francois Arago, his second main source after Laplace. Blanqui's account of the comets relies entirely on Arago's work, but this doesn't prevent him from expressing a peculiar form of disdain for his fellow-socialist. Blanqui, like most radical left-wing idealists of the nineteenth century, had quickly come to the realization that revolutionary movements (including his own) are suffering from a chronic case of what Freud would later diagnose as the "narcissism of small differences." In his courtroom defense of March 31, 1849, relative to the events of the previous year, Blanqui declares that "the closest of opinions are those that hate each other the most."[6] For such small differences mean everything, on either side of which one is an accomplice or not. For there are opinions that implicate the whole of history with them, and Arago's moderation has, according to Blanqui, made him part of a history toward which the only honest attitude was withdrawal, and flight to the margins. Arago, Blanqui believes, is one of those republicans whose success in the revolution of 1848 only led to a weak provisional government and a Second Republic (Arago resigned with his entire provisional government after 6 weeks in power, on June 24, 1848, making way for the Second Republic), a Republic which in turn would collapse into the criminal embrace of Napoleon III. To Blanqui's mind, in one of the rash shortcuts that characterize all historical materialism, Arago's Republic means Napoleon's Empire, for it came before it and remote causality counts as identity. Through a series of intellectual sleights of hand later made common knowledge by the excesses of Soviet dogmatism, Blanqui already anticipates the great materialist thesis that internality is nothing, intention and result cannot be distinguished, and the fact makes the guilt. Blanqui declares with emphasis:

> What barrier threatens the revolution of tomorrow? It is the very same barrier that wrecked the revolution of yesterday. It is the deplorable popularity of the bourgeois in orator's disguise.
>
> Ledru-Rollin, Louis Blanc, Crémieux, Marie, Lamartine, Garnier-Pagès, Dupont (de l'Eure), Flocon, Albert, Arago, Marrast!
>
> Mournful list! Sinister names! Spelled out in blood letters on all the paving stones of democratic Europe.
>
> It is the provisional government that killed the revolution! It is on its head that must fall the responsibility of all the disasters, the blood of so many thousand victims.
>
> The reaction only did its job when it slaughtered democracy. The crime belongs to the traitors whom the trusting population had accepted as their guides and who delivered the population to the reaction.[7]

Arago, the traitor, is also the main source of Blanqui's account of the comets, and yet, even as a theorist, he is represented as a member of a hubristic humankind that dismisses the comets (something that Blanqui himself does, too) with a sense of cruelty (which it seems Blanqui wants to disassociate himself from):

> Nowadays everyone has come to deeply despise those comets as miserable toys to the superior planets that rough them up, tear them apart in hundreds of ways, inflate them with solar fires, and finally throw them away in tatters. Complete degeneration! How humble

> was our former respect, when they were greeted as messengers of death! How many boos and whistles now that we know them to be harmless! There is mankind for us.

The nuance is subtle but, perhaps, significant: if Arago's results are accepted by Blanqui, it is the attitude that differs, for the sense of cruelty Blanqui wants to read in Arago's views echoes his political criticism: Bourgeois leaders cannot identify with the population they lead; in fact, they are always potential traitors for their commitment to the masses is only ever accidental. Similarly, the pleasure one may take in the spectacle of the woeful comets relies on a sense of distance, a breaking of the universal kinship of all celestial bodies in the infinite and immanent world of Blanqui's vision. Blanqui's critical relationship with Arago, like with Laplace, comes from his literal cosmo-politanism, a crucible where worlds and ages become brothers, as well as the potential, the actual, theory and practice, and with them, all disciplines; and eventually, man and nature themselves become reconciled.

For indeed, if there is any value for us—men of the twenty-first century and of a quantum world that belies Blanqui's hypothesis at every turn—in reading Blanqui nonetheless, it is not for the science, a strange mash-up of Laplace and Arago, but for reasons that are cultural in the deepest sense. Blanqui's text exerts a fascination that relies not only on the psycho-historical mystery of the hard-nosed activist turned speculative prophet, but further, in its ability to collapse the distinction of action and contemplation, and with it, that of mind and world. It is perhaps from this angle that the cases of Blanqui's illustrious readers may be best approached.

## IV

Nietzsche, with his focus on the thought of eternal recurrence as offering the ultimate reconciliation between man and reality, proposes uncanny echoes of Blanqui. Although there are allusions to it in several earlier texts, Nietzsche decided to present his thought of eternal recurrence for the first time in explicit terms in an eminently famous passage from *Thus Spoke Zarathustra* (1883–5) entitled "On the Vision and the Riddle":

> 'Stop, dwarf!' I said. 'I, or you! But I am the stronger of us two—for you do not know my abyss-deep thought! That—you would not be able to bear!' Then something happened that made me lighter: for the dwarf jumped down from my shoulder, out of curiosity! And he squatted down on a rock in front of me. But there was a gateway right where we had stopped.
>
> 'Behold this gateway, dwarf!' I continued. 'It has two faces. Two ways come together here: nobody has ever taken them to the end.
>
> 'This long lane back here: it goes on for an eternity. And that long lane out there—that is another eternity.
>
> 'They contradict themselves, these ways; they confront one another head on, and here, at this gateway, is where they come together. The name of the gateway is inscribed above it: "Moment."

'But whoever should walk farther on one of them—on and on, farther and farther: do you believe, dwarf, that these ways contradict themselves eternally?'—'All that is straight lies,' murmured the dwarf contemptuously.

'All truth is crooked; time itself is a circle.'

'You Spirit of Heaviness!' I said angrily. 'Do not make it too light and easy for yourself! Or I shall leave you squatting where you squat, Lamefoot—and I carried you up!

'Behold,' I said, 'this moment! From this gateway Moment a long eternal lane runs backward: behind us lies an eternity.

'Must not whatever among all things that can walk have walked this lane already? Must not whatever among all things that can happen have happened, and been done, and passed by already?

'And if everything has already been, what do you think, dwarf, of this moment? Must this gateway too not already—have been?

'And are not all things knotted together so tightly that this moment draws after it all things that are to come? Thus—itself as well?

'For whatever among all things *can* walk: in this long lane *out*, too—it *must* walk once more!—"[8].

Unsurprisingly, it was in the 1883 preparatory *Nachlaß* to *Zarathustra* that Nietzsche's only mention of Blanqui appears. He writes:

"A. Blanqui
l'éternité par les astres
Paris 1872" (1883, 17[73])

The entry doesn't give us much; Nietzsche seems to have simply jotted down the reference to the book, leaving it open to debate whether he had read it at all.

As early as 1898, at least, during Nietzsche's own lifetime (although dating from the time of his dementia), Henri Lichtenberger pointed out that Nietzsche's thought of the eternal recurrence of the same took place in a context that included Blanqui's pamphlet, as well as several other writings from the end of the 19th century,[9] and it would go well beyond the bounds of this introduction to discuss the width of possible sources for Nietzsche's thought and the history of its appraisal. It remains that the connections between Nietzsche's thought of eternal recurrence and Blanqui's hypothesis have been pointed out, and the possible influence of Blanqui's text discussed for a long time now, without conclusive evidence as to whether Nietzsche was influenced or not by Blanqui.

Although it would be rash to declare, as did a recent French edition of *Eternity by the Stars* (2002), as well as an inspired article by Alfred Fouillée,[10] that Blanqui's pamphlet "inspired Nietzsche for his theory of 'eternal recurrence'," it may still be of some use to draw a few of the parallels that would weigh in favor of a comparison, if not in favor of the thesis of influence.

The context of the comparison, it seems to me, must be articulated around three issues. The first, and the most general, is philosophical: how did Nietzsche's philosophical interest in the idea of eternal recurrence compare to Blanqui's? The second is cosmological: how do Nietzsche and Blanqui claim to come to the cosmological idea of recurrence? The last, with more direct bearing on the question of influence, is textual: how do Blanqui and Nietzsche's presentations of the thought compare in stylistic and textual terms? The following discussion only hopes to stand as a humble overview of the terms of the conversation one could establish between Blanqui's texts and Nietzsche's thinking. A final conclusion is well beyond our reach at this stage.

The cosmological question may be settled at once. Nietzsche and Blanqui are deeply connected by the insight that the infinite supports the identity of reality and possibility, and the collapsing of any transcendence into immanence. This holds, I believe, even if we bear in mind that Nietzsche's inspiration came, for the most part at least, from sources in thermodynamics.[11] And even if Blanqui does use some sort of Lavoisier-inspired rule of the conservation of energy, this would of course not suffice to secure a direct connection between Blanqui and thermodynamics.

Beyond this deep kinship in spirit, one should note two crucial differences between Nietzsche's and Blanqui's versions of eternal recurrence as a cosmological thesis. The first one is probably the most consequential: while Blanqui's infinite calculation relies on an atomism of matter (supported by a limited number of elements), Nietzsche's calculation is based on an atomism of energy (which he later goes on to call will to power) which ensures that the units Nietzsche is dealing with are best grasped as temporal units, that is to say, as *events*, whereas

Blanqui remains within a more classical ontology of the material object. This leads to the second difference: Blanqui's repetition, based on an infinity of space and of time, is both spatial and temporal, with an emphasis on the spatial repetition that implies that all the future and past possibilities are exhausted at any given moment, somewhere in the universe. In contrast to the precedence of space in Blanqui, Nietzsche's metaphysics of energy leads him to a cosmology of time, with "great years of becoming" (*Zarathustra*, "The Convalescent"), or "cosmic years" replacing Blanqui's multiverses, and with repetition in place of simultaneity.[12]

As regards the philosophical question, the first remark that must be made is that if Blanqui's book has a philosophical intention, it is only implicitly and indirectly so. His pamphlet is chiefly an astronomical speculation and it is only in analyzing the book as an event, that is to say, an event in Blanqui's life and an event in the history of ideas, that its philosophical import comes to light. Nietzsche, on the other hand, is at pains to present his thought as possessing an importance that shall leave no institution, no cultural habit, unchanged. In his very first outline of the eternal recurrence, Nietzsche's concerns are already those of a cultural physician:

> What shall we do with the *rest* of our lives—we who have spent the majority of our lives in the most profound ignorance? We shall *teach the teaching*—it is the most powerful means of *incorporating* [*einzuverleiben*] it in ourselves. Our kind of blessedness [*Selig-*

*keit*], as teachers of the greatest teaching. (11[141] August 1881)[13]

Nietzsche regards the thought of eternal recurrence as a thought whose effect takes place within the body of its subjects, a certain kind of "incorporation." This will remain a constant in Nietzsche's rhetoric of recurrence, only dramatized further in the later years, with expressions such as the recurrence "breaking history in two" and being a "breeding thought." This of course leads to a problem still occupying Nietzsche scholars today: to what extent should we take seriously Nietzsche's claim that eternal recurrence is a cosmological fact? It seems indeed that Nietzsche expected that through its being believed, this thought would operate a radical transformation of culture, and it would be natural for him to try to provide it with a scientific basis, with a view to increasing its persuasive power. This is quite another thing from holding eternal recurrence to be a cosmological fact and then drawing consequences, whether political, cultural, or metaphysical, from this discovery. It was famously reported by Lou Andreas-Salomé and others that, although Nietzsche came to endorse a certain version of the thought of eternal recurrence at some point in 1881, by 1882,

> The recurrence idea had not as yet become a conviction in Nietzsche's mind. But only a suspicion. He had the intention of heralding it when and if it could be proven scientifically. We exchanged a series of letters about this matter, and Nietzsche constantly expressed

> the mistaken opinion that it would be possible to win for it an indisputable basis through physics experiments. It was he who decided at that time to devote ten years of exclusive study to the natural sciences at the university of Vienna or Paris.[14]

There is no doubt therefore that the scientific aspect of eternal recurrence was always at least of some interest to Nietzsche. But, as Salomé continues, Nietzsche did not intend for his projected studies in physics to divert him from his philosophical (that is to say, cultural) project, indeed, "after ten years of absolute silence, he would—in the event that his own surmise would be substantiated, which he feared—step among people again as the teacher of the eternal recurrence."[15]

There is some degree of contrast between Nietzsche and Blanqui here. In Blanqui's case, one cannot avoid—as Benjamin did—regarding his last writing as the record of a private contemplation on the meaning of fate, perhaps even a consolation for a life of missed opportunities and for a world that shall never come to be what it ought to, unless the gap between ought and is, a gap that three revolutions had failed to bridge, should turn out to be nonexistent in the first place. Nietzsche's attitude, although it coincides with the identification of goodness with reality, is different insofar as the thought of eternal recurrence is not a private consolation, but rather a public attempt at cultural transformation. In one word, where Blanqui's hypothesis sounds like a final farewell to revolution, Nietzsche's version stands as the culmination of his own cultural revolution. The socio-cultural meanings attributed by the two men to the thought they share seem fully contrary to each other.

For Nietzsche, the intention of the thought of eternal recurrence, a "breeding thought,"[16] was to create a physical reaction in the physiology of culture. The thought of eternal recurrence would liberate mankind from any phantasy of the afterlife, of so-called backworlds whose intrinsic values justify that we sacrifice the world to them, and teach us to debunk the constant sacrificial impulses of our degenerate life in favor of a life made of moments whose purpose is immanent to them, those moments that we may willfully long to see recur forever.

Further, although he too conflates actuality with possibility, Nietzsche seems to be doing so as a reduction of the possible to the actual (as a tool against what he calls the "backworlds" and the "point of view of desirability") whereas Blanqui extrapolates the actual into the range of the potential, by way of a general attribution of actuality to the entire range of the potential. It is as a result of this, it seems to me, that even if the concept of the infinite accommodates for both at the same time, Nietzsche insists on repetition, whereas Blanqui insists on variation.

In addition, it seems that by the time of *Eternity by the Stars*, the project of cultural education has almost entirely disappeared from Blanqui's focus (with the exception of his insistence that the education of cosmography is an antidote to superstition). If his letters reveal a whimsical keenness on the book, it is always a matter of having it affect the outcome of his legal appeal, and so, not by emphasizing the radicality of his own thought (while it constitutes the heart of Nietzsche's keenness on his own thought) but, on the contrary, by showing that he doesn't represent a threat to society any longer and that his thinking in *Eternity by the Stars* is now "very remote from political matters and moderate in every way."[17]

So much for the differences. They cannot help the fact that what Nietzsche finds in his own thought of eternal recurrence is also present in Blanqui's *Eternity by the Stars*. This is due, as was mentioned in discussing Blanqui's opposition to Laplace, to the centrality attributed to the notion of the infinite. Like Blanqui, Nietzsche believes that recurrence is a direct consequence of the discrepancy between possible events and the infinity of time. Like Blanqui, Nietzsche maintains such a discrepancy by assuming that the extensive infinite of time (or space), is not matched by the intensive infinite of events themselves (i.e., combinations of material entities). In different ways, Blanqui and Nietzsche are both atomists. Nietzsche shares the idea that the extensive infinite is not matched by the intensive infinite, that the infinitely large exists but not the infinitely small (as shown by Georg Simmel, who based his critique of the thought of eternal recurrence on this point as early as 1907).[18] Whether this common atomism commits both men to materialism in the same sense is a matter of discussion that would take us too far into Nietzsche's metaphysics, which is ambi-guous in precisely this respect, the question of the materiality of the will to power.[19]

Secondly, the cosmology of the infinite allows both thinkers to reject any notion of externality, or at least to reframe it as an internal difference. Nietzsche thus triumphs over his passionately reviled backworlds, and Blanqui finds that anarchism was always already achieved, although it now must be detached from socialist and revolutionary ideals: as Rancière points out in his introduction to a recent French edition of *Eternity by the Stars*, the universe is anarchic because its forces are not organized by anything but themselves.[20]

Rejecting any externality of course amounts to affirming the impossibility for any extraneous disruption to the established order, and we can only disagree with Abensour and Pelosse when they write that "Blanqui conceives of history under the form of the jump and the caesura"[21] if they intend this remark to apply even to the text of 1872. Indeed, Blanqui never sounds as tragic as when he feigns to be reluctantly taken to the conclusion that human improvement never leads outside of this world, by the force of his own arguments. His new hypothesis, he writes:

> is not much in the way of satisfying our thirst for improvement. What can we do? I haven't sought my pleasure; I have sought the truth. There is no revelation here; there is no prophet. There is nothing more than a simple deduction drawn from spectral analysis and Laplace's cosmology. These two discoveries make us eternal. Is it a blessing? Let us enjoy it. Is it a disappointment? Let us resign ourselves.

Like Blanqui, who laments the death of progress (read: socialist progress), Nietzsche "feared," in Salomé's words, that his idea might be right, for it carries within it the death of hope.

Indeed, it seems that both Blanqui and Nietzsche are committed to some sort of determinism, that is to say, at least to some idea that the possible and the necessary are equivalent (Nietzsche calls this unity "fate"). Blanqui goes even further and, by appealing to the infinity of space, establishes that necessity is also equi-valent to the actual.

We may now return to the textual question. Although the *Nachlaß* entry quoted earlier cannot substantiate much, it suggests at least that Nietzsche was aware of the general contents of Blanqui's book and probably, of its relevance to eternal recurrence. In fact, it is most likely that 1883 was not Nietzsche's first encounter with Blanqui's text. In Nietzsche's beloved *History of Materialism*, which he first read upon its publication in 1866 (as well as in 1868, 1873, 1881, 1884, 1885, and possibly in 1883),[22] Lange refers to Blanqui's work in a footnote. He writes:

> It is interesting that recently a Frenchman (A. Blanqui, *L'éternité par les astres, hypothèse astronomique*, Paris, 1872) has carried out again, quite seriously, the idea that everything possible is somewhere and at some time, realized in the universe, and in fact, has often been realized, and that as an inevitable consequence, on the one hand, of the absolute infinity of the universe, but on the other, of the very finite and

> everywhere constant number of the elements, whose possible combinations, must also be finite. This last is also an idea of Epikuros (Comp. Lucretius, ii, 480–521).[23]

This note of Lange's appears on page 107 in the German edition owned by Nietzsche. However, it must be noted that the footnote was only added in the second edition of Lange's book from 1873 (one year after the publication of Blanqui's pamphlet). Although this is also one of the years that Nietzsche re-read the book, Thomas H. Brobjer reports that it was only in his re-reading of 1884 that Nietzsche can be said with certainty to have read a later edition of Lange's book (in this case, the 4th edition of 1882). In this context, we might ask why the usually thorough Brobjer fails to mention which edition Nietzsche may have read in 1883, probably due to his basic supposition that Nietzsche's note in the *Nachlaß* is inspired by Lange.[24] Of course, if it could be shown that, before 1884, Nietzsche had in fact no access to any edition of Lange's book other than the first, this would indicate that he heard of Blanqui through some other channel, perhaps even through direct reading.

So much for the facts. And clearly, the facts are inconclusive, calling for careful speculation. What follows are some indications of points that might usefully feed into such speculations, with the proviso that it be remembered that no conclusion may as yet be drawn with any degree of certainty. Until the scholarship provides us with definite facts, I would like to point out a number of stylistic devices in

Nietzsche that are strikingly reminiscent of Blanqui's language in *Eternity by the Stars*, both in literary and conceptual terms.

Both in his *Nachlaß* of 1873 (a year after the publication of *Eternity* and on the year of Lange's second edition, the one that included references to Blanqui), and later, Nietzsche notes that the infinite variations of each other that different men represent, sometimes gives rise to those he calls the "philosopher" and shall later call the "lucky strokes [*Glücksfälle*]."[25] They are random appearances for whom we must thank the grand calculus of infinity, because, as Nietzsche shall maintain throughout his career, nature is a poor economist, it "propels the philosopher into mankind like an arrow, it takes no aim but hopes it will stick somewhere," incurring astounding wastage.[26] These lucky strokes, Nietzsche repeats, are our only hope, for the fact of eternal recurrence makes progress a meaningless term. On the contrary, our hope cannot be in any future or general improvement, but only in some lucky variation, and Nietzsche never uses the term *Glücksfälle* in any other context than a criticism of progress from the point of view of recurrence and the subsequent quest for an object of longing that would not rely on any concept of progress.[27] This object, for Nietzsche, is precisely the lucky stroke, or in more famously Nietzschean language: the Overhuman. In a late *Nachlaß* entry entitled "*Übermensch*," he writes:

> Mankind does not exhibit any evolution towards the better, or the stronger, or the superior: in the sense

given to such words nowadays: the European man of the 19th century is, in term of his value, much inferior to the Europeans of the Renaissance; the pursuit of evolution has absolutely nothing to do with necessity, elevation, intensification of reinforcement... In another sense there exists a constant *success* of special cases on different corners of the earth, and springing from different cultures, in whom *a superior type presents itself*: something that, with regard to the whole of mankind is some sort of an "overhuman" [*Übermensch*]. Such cases of luck and great success have always been possible and shall probably always be so. And even tribes, generations, and entire peoples may turn out to represent such *lucky strokes* [*Glücksfälle*]. (11 [413] 1888, see also *Anti-Christ* §4. Nietzsche's emphasis.)

Blanqui, much more succinctly and with probably less prophetic insight, seems to propose the same organization of eternal recurrence, infinite variations, and the preclusion of progress and hope: all we can hope for now are, he writes, "lucky variations" ("*des variantes heureuses*"):

Yet, there is one shortcoming: there is no progress. Alas! no, these are vulgar reissues, repetitions. So too are the copies of past worlds, so too are those of future worlds. Only the chapter of bifurcations remains open to hope. [...] Men of the 19th century, the hour of our appearance is fixed once and for all, and always assigns us the same incarnation. At best, it gives us the perspective of lucky variations ["*des variantes heureuses*"].

All the above parallels have to do with the calculus of probabilities that Blanqui and Nietzsche share, and most of them with *Zarathustra*, the text of the Eternal Recurrence itself. A second remark might be made about a section of *Zarathustra*, entitled "On Great Events." The general motif of that section is the discrepancy between the importance given by humans to themselves and not only their indifference in the eyes of the rest of the universe, but even their despicable aspect. The rhetorical device is powerful: we humans take ourselves (our history, our species, and its fate) seriously and this taking seriously is supported by the delusion that we have an importance that is objectively acknowledged, that is, an importance that is not merely self-attributed. Placing ourselves before the awareness of the fact that mankind is a matter of indifference to all that is not human is, in typically Nietzschean fashion, a way of placing us before our contradictions: we think we are more important than nature (or, Nietzsche says in less allegorical texts, God) but we make nature the judge of our own importance. In Nietzsche's (and Blanqui's) mind: we gain our feeling of superiority as a derivation of our feeling of inferiority insofar as it is to the so-called inferior that we bestow the right to anoint us.

Nietzsche-Zarathustra continues: in fact, it is only within the human realm that human matters are of any consequence, and the same anthropocentrism is at play in our obsession with politics: "the state is a hypocritical hound [...,] it likes to speak with smoke and bellowing—so as to make believe [...] that it speaks from the belly of things. For it wants to be by all means the most important beast on earth, the state."[28]

Again, the idols of the human tribe are laughable from the perspective of the whole, and in fact, all the sound and fury—for the great events, Zarathustra declares, are silent—of human history makes mankind a mere rash on the surface of the earth. Zarathustra opens his speech by declaring: "the earth has a skin and this skin has diseases, one of these diseases is called, for example, humanity" (ibid.).

Blanqui seems to have inaugurated the same metaphor in the same context. After repeatedly insisting—like Zarathustra—that noisy events are by nature human and therefore unimportant and that great events happen "noiselessly" and "peacefully"[29] he writes:

> Men do not disturb matter very much, but they disturb themselves a great deal. The turbulences of man never affect the natural workings of the physical phenomena in any serious manner, but they do turn their own kind upside down. We must therefore factor in this subversive influence that changes the course of individual destinies, destroys and modifies the animal species, tears nations apart, and collapses empires. Of course, all this violence takes place without *leaving as much as a scratch on the skin of the earth.* [My emphasis]

A perhaps more striking parallel might be found closer to Zarathustra and Blanqui's explicit expositions of recurrence. In Nietzsche's most seminal elaboration of his thought, the section entitled "On the Vision and the Riddle," Zarathustra is at pains to ensure that eternal recurrence is properly understood as the eternal recurrence *of the same*. For one to pass the test, Zarathustra insists, he must will for every last detail to recur forever again. Every last detail, that is to say, also "this slow moving spider, crawling in the moonlight, and this moonlight itself."

Zarathustra only provides two examples of the details that are so important in understanding the thought of eternal recurrence, and for myself, I do find the choice of the spider to be—although deeply poetic—unexpected. It is, of course, the choice made by Blanqui in his own text, perhaps more understandably, as Blanqui insists on the threads of the spider's web—reminiscent of the "hairy nihilities" of the comets—as examples of infinitely small objects that nonetheless take part in the cosmic repetition:

> Hence the billions of earths, absolutely identical both personally and materially, where neither a blade of hay nor a thousandth second, nor a spider's thread vary in either time or space.

The final passage I wish to focus on is perhaps more significant theoretically as well as stylistically:

Blanqui writes: "The mere fact that any celestial body exists now proves that it has always existed." And Nietzsche in 1888: "If the motion of the world aimed at a final state, that state would have been reached."[30]

Blanqui writes:

> All of these earths stumble, one after the other, into the rejuvenating flames, so as to be born again and to stumble again, in the monotonous flow of an hourglass eternally turning itself over and emptying itself. What we have is ever-old newness and ever-new oldness.

And Nietzsche:

> You teach that there is a Great Year of Becoming, a monster of a Great Year, which must like an hourglass turn itself over anew, again and again, that it may run down and run out ever anew.
>
> (*Zarathustra*, "The Convalescent" 193)

And a few entries after his first written reference to eternal recurrence in the *Nachlaß* of 1881:

> The world of the forces suffers no decrease: since otherwise it would have become weak in the infinite time and would have disappeared. *The world of forces suffers no standstill: since, otherwise, it would have been reached*, and the clock of existence ticks along quietly. The world of the forces never comes to a balance, it never has a moment of peace, its force and movement are equally strong at any given moment. Whatever condition this world can reach, it must have reached it before and not just once, but innumerable times. So this moment: it already took place once and many other times before, and it will return as well, and all forces shall distribute themselves just so, and every moment links up with the moment that bore it and with the next which is its offspring. *Man! Your whole*

> *life will be turned like an hourglass* [*Sanduhr*] *again and run out again*—a big minute of time in between, since all conditions from which you have become, in the cycle of the world, will be gathered again. And then you shall find again every pain and every desire and every friend and enemy and every hope and every error and *every blade of grass* and every gaze into the sun, the whole connection of all things. *This ring in which you are a grain shines again.* And in every ring of human existence as such there is always an hour in which there emerges, at first for one, then for many, the most powerful thought emerges then to all from the eternal return of all things—it is every time for mankind the hour of the noon. (11[148] 1881)

Similarly in a reworked version of the same passage published in the *Gay Science* of 1882, he declares:

> What if a demon crept after you into your loneliest loneliness some day or night, and said to you: "This life, as you live it at present, and have lived it, you must live it once more, and also innumerable times; and there will be nothing new in it, but every pain and every joy and every thought and every sigh, and all the unspeakably small and great in your life must come to you again, and all in the same series and sequence and similarly *this spider and this moonlight among the trees,* and similarly this moment, and I myself. *The eternal sand glass* [*Sanduhr*] *of existence will ever be turned once more, and you with it, you speck of dust!*" Would you not throw yourself down and gnash your teeth, and curse the demon that spoke thus? *Or* have you once experienced a tremendous

> moment in which you wouldst answer him: "you are a God, and never did I hear anything so divine!" If that thought acquired power over you as you are, it would transform you, and perhaps crush you; the question with regard to all and everything: "Do you want this once more, and also for innumerable times?" would lie as the heaviest burden upon your activity! Or, how would you have to become favorably inclined to yourself and to life, so as to long for nothing more ardently than for this ultimate sanction and seal?" (*The Gay Science* §341)

The metaphor of the hourglass, remarkably well chosen for the purpose of exposing the existential implications of the idea of recurrence, seems therefore to be shared by Blanqui and Nietzsche, but there is more: the context of this echo only feeds further into the parallel for, of all the many different implications Nietzsche extracts from the idea of eternal recurrence, all of those that echo Blanqui's account are found unified here: the hourglass appears in the vicinity of the spider discussed above, the "blade of grass" echoes Blanqui's "blade of hay" from the same quotation, and the idea of resurrection associated with the hourglass (an association which Nietzsche makes even more directly in a draft to *Zarathustra*)[31] and all of them are connected with the idea, crucial for both Nietzsche and Blanqui, that no standstill (or origin) is possible, because its mere possibility would make the present impossible. Finally, Nietzsche's existential framing of the question seems to echo Blanqui's own psychological questioning (his only diversion from his scientific tone) in a passage already cited:

> What can we do? I haven't sought my pleasure; I have sought the truth. There is no revelation here, nor prophet, but a simple deduction drawn from spectral analysis and the cosmology of Laplace. These two discoveries make us eternal. Is it a blessing? Let us take advantage of it. Is it a mystification? Let us resign ourselves.

Like Nietzsche, whose philosophical genius is able to follow the consequences of this alternative down to the duality of Turkish and Russian fatalism, of active and passive nihilism, and to finally discover the selective power of the thought of eternal recurrence, Blanqui recognizes that the thought of recurrence leaves us with an alternative: it compels us to decide whether it brings "blessings" or "resignation." For this choice, Nietzsche declares, is indeed the "heaviest burden."

Do these surprising intertextual parallels suffice to demonstrate an influence of the present text on Nietzsche's writing (and perhaps his thinking)? Surely not. Indeed, it seems that every single one of these instances, taken separately, may be explained away quite well without postulating that Nietzsche even read Blanqui. It is only taken together that they amount to some sort of substantiation. I have no further purpose than to present some of the passages that would gain clarification should Nietzsche's knowledge of Blanqui ever be confirmed, and perhaps, to suggest that since the matter is inconclusive either way, the possibility that Nietzsche was struck by Blanqui's textual idiosyncrasies may be kept in mind alongside the possibility that we are before one of the many striking intellectual coincidences of the nineteenth century.

## V

In contemporary times, the philosophical honor of Blanqui was championed almost single-handedly by Walter Benjamin. A cultural historian, that is to say, a cultural physician, Benjamin was struck by such coincidences between Nietzsche and Blanqui, and in general, by the recurrence of a certain set of patterns throughout the Great European tradition, among them the idea of repetition, recurrence, and of an all-encompassing cosmos.[32] He seems to have encountered Blanqui's text for the first time late in 1937[33] and included several long quotes from the text and a host of commentaries on it in his second "presentation" of his unfinished *Arcades* project. There, he quotes Nietzsche's declaration according to which ends were impossible (because the eternity of past time means they would have been reached) in connection to an extensive quotation from Blanqui.[34] The pattern of recurrence itself, he points out, seems to recur in uncanny ways across Baudelaire, Blanqui, and Nietzsche (and presumably Heine and others too), all of them unified by their "*idée fixe* of the new and the immutable."[35]

Benjamin's interest in Blanqui's cosmological hypothesis seems to feed into several of his general projects, namely, to demonstrate the connections between Baudelaire and radical socialism to elucidate the nature of the nineteenth century as a confession of modernity's true essence, and to pursue his critique of historicism.[36]

As regards Baudelaire, the unfinished writings seem to provide only a number of declarations of principles on Benjamin's part, but although his declared objective is to "make the effort to bring to light" Blanqui's "obscure and profound relationship to Baudelaire, whom it almost literally echoes in some splendid passages,"[37] the texts establishing any sort of direct connection between Blanqui and Baudelaire remain scarce.[38] It remains that Benjamin's intuition, which saw Baudelaire and Blanqui as two aspects of each other, indeed, as a Siamese pair, with "Blanqui's action the sister of Baudelaire's dream,"[39] could only be fascinated to see Blanqui's last text unifying in unexpected (and to Benjamin's mind, disappointing) ways, the face of action with the face of the dream:

> Show with maximum force how the idea of eternal recurrence emerged at about the same time in the worlds of Baudelaire, Blanqui, and Nietzsche. In Baudelaire, the accent is on the new, which is wrested with heroic effort from the 'ever-selfsame';. in Nietzsche, it is on the 'ever-selfsame,' which the human being faces with heroic composure. Blanqui is far closer to Nietzsche than to Baudelaire; but in his work, resignation predominates. In Nietzsche, this experience is projected onto a cosmological plane, in his thesis that nothing

new will occur. ("Central Park," *Essays on Baudelaire* 151).

Indeed, Benjamin's hermeneutics of modernity regards the triad of Baudelaire's hallucinatory dream-world, Blanqui's *Eternity*, and Nietzsche's *Zarathustra* as all pointing to two correlated events: the drying up of meaning in history and the self-determination of modernity as awareness. Benjamin's first approach of eternal recurrence is made from the perspective of its mythic potential, as the idea of recurrence turns the "course of the world" into "one great allegory,"[40] but it should not be misunderstood as an affirmation of meaning, for it is only as a consolation that recurrence provides allegory and myth. For Benjamin, of course, the question is to determine what the consolation is for, and the answer is almost immediate, the consolation is for the absence of meaning. For Benjamin—just like Foucault later—recognizes that circularity is the emblem of modernity much more decisively than the structure of the universe. History loses meaning inasmuch as it is now seen to be unable of bringing creation, that is to say, a renewal in the experience of living. Likewise, in this inability to project itself towards a qualitative future, it becomes aware of itself as failure. For Benjamin, the common project of Baudelaire, Blanqui, and Nietzsche is indeed to use this awareness of failure as an unheard-of event that transforms modernity into a ceaselessly self-regenerating awareness of itself as sterile: Blanqui insists in a phrase that Benjamin cherished, that, "As men of the $19^{th}$ century, the hour of our appearance is fixed once and for all, and it always assigns us the same incarnation at best." Even if, "At heart, man's eternity by the stars is melancholic. Even sadder is this estrangement of the twin-worlds caused by the inexorable barrier of space. So many identical populations go by without suspecting each other's existence! Well, not really: this shared existence is found again in the nineteenth century. But who shall believe it?"

There, it seems, Blanqui tears the veil of repetition in order to stand, even if whimsically, outside of the cycle he describes, for this description itself—as meaning if not as physical act—can only be conceived as a great event (indeed, it is this event, the *telling* of uneventfulness, that Nietzsche himself developed into a thought able to break the history of mankind in two). But, Benjamin declares, these men of the nineteenth century can only be invoked as "apparitions" coming from the "regions" of "hell."[41] For "hell" becomes Benjamin's name for a nineteenth century[42] that no longer projects itself towards the future, for the arousal of self-awareness only counts as resignation, and condemns us to reproducing objects in our longing for meanings that are now lost. The repetition that Benjamin sees disclosed in Blanqui's last text is only a statement of disappointed resignation, a surrender of the revolutionary to his prison guards, and the reversal of his historical energy into a flight into the skies that bears no resemblance to the heavens but rather, a flight that designs the cosmic space as the space of hell. For hell is closure for Benjamin, and the infinite of space and time should not be regarded as openness but as a constantly self-exhausting universe, a prison indeed. The imprisoned Blanqui, in Benjamin's view, resembles no one more than the imprisoned "blonde beast" of Nietzsche's *Genealogy of Morality*, one who finds inner space when outer action is now impossible, one who sublimates action into thinking, but whose thinking can never project itself outside of its own *raison d'être*: resigned thinking can only think resignation. As Benjamin seems to intuit in a striking note from the *Arcades*, his project will have to

> pursue the question of whether a connection exists between the secularization of time in space [with its disappointing preclusion of progress] and the allegorical mode of perception [which, as Nietzsche shows, results from the imprisonment induced by this inability to believe in progress any longer]. The former at any rate (as becomes clear in Blanqui's last writing), is hidden in the 'worldview of the natural sciences' of the second half of the century. (*Arcades* 472)

And, echoing Nietzsche's claim that such imprisonment leads to poetic thinking (or, in Benjamin's words, "allegorical perception"), that is to say, the offsetting of warlike instincts by way of transformation into the symbolic realm, Benjamin notes in the context of "studying the allegorical work of Baudelaire" how the poet proposes:

> a Blanquist look at the terrestrial globe: 'I contemplate from on high the globe in its rondure, / and I no longer seek the shelter of a hut ("Le Goût du Néant").

The poet has made his dwelling in space itself, one could say, or in the abyss. (*Arcades* 352)

Like Nietzsche, Benjamin sees the healing power of the thought of eternal recurrence in helping to rid us of the fantasy of progress. For after all, the only "disappointment" contained in Blanqui's conclusion is the mourning of progress. Benjamin writes: "Blanqui's cosmic speculation conveys this lesson: that humanity will be prey to a mythic anguish so long as phantasmagoria occupies a place in it."[43]

Here we can find a beginning of explanation regarding Benjamin's ambiguous understanding of Blanqui's cosmological confinement. If it is true that *Eternity by the Stars* presents an *a priori* critique of any notion of progress, it is also by offering at this very instant a way out of the locking up of history. For what Benjamin sees emerging from the musings of Blanqui is the opening up of the space of discourse as the renewed space of history. After all, the realm of meaning is not subjected to the material restrictions of atomism and the elemental constitution of the world, and the taking possession of this realm by the human is never better exemplified than by the liberating force of the awareness of confinement. When Blanqui claims that the truth of the cosmos has been recuperated in the nineteenth century by himself, the momentous event is precisely that the awareness of the cosmological fact breaks it at this very minute, it is the recognition that no cosmological model could account for the act of a lone mind that tells it: the telling of closure is the liberation from closure, or as Benjamin, writes: "abyss."

So, if Benjamin recognizes that Blanqui's pamphlet amounts indeed to a capitulation on the part of the revolutionary, it is because his revolutionary struggle was precisely always fought in the material mode: injustice was a material organization, that is to say, ultimately, an organization of atoms. Yet, Benjamin declares mysteriously that Blanqui's hypothesis does not preclude re-volution. That is to say, a further revolution, one that is conceived as the removal of injustice, may be maintained, if injustice becomes properly understood as taking place in the realm of meaning, that is to say, the realm of historical action, in a philosophy of history that removes itself from materialism. For the realm of meaning, if not fetishized into "myth,"—that is, if not naively taken to denote and depend on a material state of affairs—retains its human, that is to say, political, potential. This is the "good" meaning of modernity as a liberation from the material, which wrests us from myth and enters us into allegory, the human mode of meaning. Perhaps the most intimate connection between Blanqui and Baudelaire in Benjamin is one left implicit in his own working notes:

> A question to be reserved until the end: How is it possible that a stance seemingly so 'untimely' as allegory should have taken such a prominent place in the poetic work of the century? Allegory should be shown as the antidote to myth. Myth was the comfortable route from which Baudelaire abstained. A poem like "La vie anterieure": whose very title invites every sort of compromise, shows how far removed Baudelaire was from

myth. End with the Blanqui quotation, "Hommes du dix-neuvième siècle." ("Central Park," *Essays on Baudelaire* 154–5.)

It is with this summoning of the men of the day, Benjamin believes, that Blanqui tears the veil of materiality and redefines modernity as the age characterised by the allegorical world of human freedom. The cosmological hypothesis becomes regarded as the great humanizing thought. With this thought, Blanqui takes place within this paradoxical reading of infinity as closure, as the space in which history just hits its head against the limits of the cosmos, for the repetition is nothing but the repetition of the bruising experience of imprisonment. Benjamin declares that the cosmic extrapolation of the infinity that offers repetition contained in Blanqui and Nietzsche is nothing other than an industrialization of the cosmos, it is the knot in which modern nihilism, self-awareness, the drying up of meaningful (or qualitative) history and the correlative drying up of "the aura" in the industrial age find their mutual kinship. To return to Benjamin's mythic interpretation of recurrence, we may now see how, although it is true that "life within the magic circle of eternal return makes for an existence that never emerges from the auratic,"[44] it is also true that such life is made impossible by the very awareness of recurrence, which tears it apart, and it is clear that the invocation of the "men of the 19th century" is nothing but the declaration that the making visible of recurrence means the overcoming of the myth, the very emergence shatters the auratic and truly introduces us to the world of mechanical reproduction. It is precisely here that Blanqui and Baudelaire collide, in the frightening observation of the terrestrial globe, the emergence from the mythical embeddedness of man in world, and the human ability to look at his own cosmos as an object. Heidegger's famous shock in seeing the pictures of the earth from the sky has its origins in Baudelaire and Blanqui:[45]

> Neurosis creates the mass-produced article in the psychic economy. There it takes the form of the obsessional idea, which, manufactured in countless copies, appears in the household of the neurotic mind as the ever selfsame. Conversely, in Blanqui, the idea of eternal return itself takes the form of an obsessional idea. The idea of eternal recurrence transforms the historical event itself into a mass-produced article. But this conception also displays, in another respect—on its obverse side, one could say—a trace of the economic circumstances to which it owes its sudden topicality. This was manifest at the moment the security of the conditions of life was considerably diminished through an accelerated succession of crises. The idea of eternal recurrence derived its luster from the fact that it was no longer possible, in all circumstances, to expect a recurrence of conditions across any interval of time shorter than that provided by eternity. The recurrence of quotidian constellations became gradually less frequent and there could arise, in consequence, the obscure presentiment that henceforth one must rest content with cosmic constellations. Habit, in short, made ready to surrender some of its

> prerogatives. Nietzsche says, 'I love short-lived habits' and before this, Baudelaire was throughout his life incapable of developing regular habits. ("Central Park," *Essays on Baudelaire* 140)

Effectively, it seems Benjamin and Nietzsche would agree that the lesson of Blanqui's hypothesis lies precisely in the fact that in trying to recuperate itself, that is in trying to recuperate the telling of the hypothesis of recurrence. Circularity now names a world that contains its own self-awareness as a determination of its own esence.

## VI

We can now see how it happened—through a historical coincidence that Benjamin's genius would probably have much to say about—that in the very years of Benjamin's engagement with Blanqui, Jorge-Luis Borges became enthralled with *Eternity by the Stars* for reasons directly related to his practical and ongoing ontology of fiction. For Borges, it was all too clear how the unification of all the possibles within the grand whole of infinity meant the vanishing of the difference between text and reality. As Lisa Block de Behar notes, the idea of eternal recurrence is

> constant as well in the imaginary of Borges: "Tlön, Uqbar, Orbis Tertius," "The South," "The Theologians," "The Other Death," "The Library of Babel," "The Garden of Forking Paths." "Death and the Compass," and so many more, the duplications and

> dualities could only be explained partially if not for the vision of alternative worlds enabled by and inhabited by the fabulous cosmogony of Blanqui.[46]

In the appropriately titled section of 1936's *History of Eternity* called "Circular Time," Borges writes that

> all principles of eternal return [*eterno regreso*] were justified by "an algebraic principle," and only the objects counted varied, not the principle: for Plato, it was an "astrological" calculus, Du Bon was counting "atoms," Nietzsche "forces" and "the communist Blanqui" "simple bodies." Whatever the object, all these theorists admit that these objects were "unable to make up an infinite number of variations."[47]

And even if the "best reasoned of these three doctrines is Blanqui's," whose "book, beautifully entitled *L'éternité par les astres*, is from 1872,"[48] this doesn't mean that Borges grants Blanqui the last word.

A few years later, in the famous "Library of Babel" (1941), Borges returns to Blanqui, albeit implicitly. In the legendary library, all possible 410-page books of a given format are held, allowing Borges to take the final step in the variations on the eternal recurrence inherited from the nineteenth century: for atoms, forces, and simple bodies must be complemented with the most momentous of all units: "orthographic symbols." One of the books, for example, is written in an unknown language. Some think it is Portuguese, some Yiddish, and after a century of research, it is established to be some—conceivable, that is to say, real—language best described as a "Samoyedo-Lithuanian dialect of Guarani, with some inflexions of Classical Arabic,"[49] and with the language the contents themselves become revealed:

> Notions of combinatory analysis, illustrated with examples of variations and unlimited repetition. It was those examples that allowed a librarian of genius to discover the fundamental law of the library. This thinker observed that all the books, although diverse, all contained equal elements: the space, the period, the comma, the twenty-two letters of the alphabet. He even uncovered a fact confirmed by all the travelers: that there wasn't, in the vast library, two identical books. From these undisputable premises, he deduced that the library was total and that its shelves contained all the possible combinations of the twenty-something orthographic symbols (their number was, although extremely great, not infinite).
>
> (*Obras completas* 467)

In the cosmos that is the library, any book is a world and the book that teaches of this recurrence is only referring to itself as one world among others and to the others as variations of itself. When Blanqui writes his book, Borges seems to suggest, he also makes the ontological claim that all books and their contents are of the same reality. He is himself astounded at the relations between language and possibility, for the flip side of the inadequacy of language in expressing the infinite ("one cannot fondle the infinite with words") is that all that can be said must be real too, and the simultaneity between the saying of the possible and its actuality resembles the act of creation itself: "let us not be alarmed at those globes pouring out of the quill by the billions," let us not be alarmed by our own godly power in which conceiving and creating become one. Instead, Borges finds in Blanqui "the possibilities of connection between the parallel worlds favored by fiction."[50] In this context, Blanqui's cosmic extrapolation of the powers of the quill can only resonate strongly with Borges who, in one of his most famous prose poems, describes a Blanqui-like prisoner, as the other self of all authors, the promethean figure who not only writes replicas—as all writings are—but who also writes of replication:

> In a deserted part of Iran there is a not-so tall tower of stone, without doors or windows. In the one room (whose floor is of dirt and which has the shape of a circle) there is a table of wood and a bench. In that circular cell, a man who looks like me writes in characters that I do not understand a long poem about a man in another circular cell who writes a poem about a man who in another circular cell... The process has no end and no one will be able to read what the prisoners write.

For Borges, Blanqui's hypothesis constitutes the tearing up of replication and through this tear, the entire world of symbolic replication rushes in: finally, we become able to "read what the prisoners write" for, thanks to Blanqui, the process is momentarily interrupted, in a moment that gives birth to modernity.

> At heart, man's eternity by the stars is melancholic, and even sadder this estrangement of brother-worlds caused by the inexorable barrier of space. So many identical populations come to pass without having suspected each other's existence! Well, not really: this shared existence is discovered at last in the 19th century. But who shall believe it?

Finally, we become able to read what the prisoner writes.

## VII

Such is the creative power of what Blanqui calls the "quill," that by speaking of the world the quill lets the world speak. Blanqui regards writing, the stars, and universal cycles to have a common essence: they reflect each other endlessly: they write the text that the writer reads. For Blanqui, the text is a story of a stellar repetition that becomes ceaselessly disrupted by writing: together, stars and word represent the way in which reality leads outside of itself, the way that reality makes room within itself for meaning, the way reality offers some of its inhabitants a way out of itself, into the world of culture and of text. Mother nature is only a mother if it allows her children to be born, like Menaechmi, Blanqui says, we humans are brothers and so are the many worlds that a now fertile universe is bringing forth endlessly.

It is universal brotherhood that motivates the revolution Blanqui calls for. Indeed, the pen and the world have a common master: love that doesn't know how to separate, love within which all worlds are brothers, says Blanqui.

But the awareness of this fact changes everything, for it makes the brotherhood real: "So many identical populations go by without suspecting each other's existence! Well, not really: this shared existence is found again in the nineteenth century. But who shall believe it?" This is the privilege of the creative revolutionary, both cultural and political: understanding the resources offered by the paradox of writing: the innocent act of telling the world as it is, is doubled out with the revolutionary act of making it what it ought to be.

For if Blanqui's short book is a tragic meditation about the power of destiny, it is also a rejoinder about the freedom that emanates from it. To the militant, this rejoinder is a call to action. To the reader, it is an invitation to deconstruct his own fatalism. The paradoxes of this little book are the paradoxes of modernity. Made of a ceaseless mixture of fraudulent freedom and fraudulent determinism, modernity endlessly disappoints and compels us. Constantly, Blanqui insists on the material character of the world and on the infinite necessity it entails. And constantly, he defeats his own point, stumbles on his own words. He describes a world with no meaning, a world of atoms which would make reading, translating, and understanding an aberration, but immediately, his quill tears apart the garb of necessity even as he draws it upon himself. He scolds himself: "well, not really..."

Blanqui's mixture of fatalism and activism has its place within a chain that links him, in the past, with the Anatolian mystic Yunus Emre, Shakespeare, and Hegel, but also with the nameless army of authors of ex votos and devotional writings, and after him, with Nietzsche, Proust, Benjamin, and Borges. Alongside them, Blanqui's text is the stage where fate and writing enter their endless dance of seduction and combat. It reminds us, in all its tensions, that even though the written life is different from the unwritten one, writing does not bring forth more than ink splatters. But such is the magic of the human power of escaping necessity; that is measured by the infinite nihility that separates a letter from the paper it touches. For it is physics that liberates us from matter, astronomy that liberates us from the stars, and tragedy that liberates us from the tragic.

Blanqui too understood in the age of industrialization: it is only the impossible mixture of meaning and matter, only their unstable but necessary coexistence that can lead us to the productive, human future we seek. We must pursue neither the mysticism of materialism nor the cruelty of pure spiritualism, but only the human vocation to introduce meaning within matter.

# Eternity by the Stars

## An Astronomical Hypothesis

## I. The Universe—the Infinite

The universe is infinite in time and space, eternal, boundless and undivided. All physical bodies, animate and inanimate, solid, liquid and gaseous, are held together by the very things that separate them. Everything holds together. If one removed the celestial bodies, space would remain, absolutely empty of course, but still possessing all three dimensions, length, width, and depth, space undivided and unlimited.

Pascal once said in his magnificent language: "The universe is a circle, whose center is everywhere and its circumference nowhere."[51] What more striking image can present the infinite? Let us be even more precise and say after him: The universe is a sphere, whose center is everywhere and its surface nowhere.

The universe lies before us, open to observation and to reason. An incalculable number of stars shine from within its depths. Let us think of ourselves as standing in one of these "sphere centers," which are everywhere, and whose surface is nowhere, and assume for a moment the existence of this surface, lying at the edge of the world.

Shall we say that this edge is solid, liquid, or gaseous? Whatever its nature, it immediately becomes the prolongation of what it restricts or attempts to restrict. Let us assume that at this point in space, there exists nothing solid, nothing liquid, no gas, not even ether. Nothing but space, void and dark.

This space is not deprived of a third dimension however, and its limit, that is to say, its continuation, will lie in a new portion of space of the same nature, and thereafter, in another, then another still, and so on, *indefinitely*.

The infinite can only present itself to us as an aspect of the *indefinite*. The one leads into the other by virtue of our manifest inability to encounter or even conceive of any limitation in space. Of course, the infinite universe is incomprehensible, but the limited universe is absurd. Our absolute certainty that the world is infinite, combined with its incomprehensibility, constitutes one of the most frustrating annoyances that torment the human spirit. There exists, undoubtedly, somewhere in the wandering globes, some brains whose vigor succeeds in grasping an enigma so impenetrable to ours. Let our jealousy come to terms with it.

The enigma is the same whether one considers the infinite in time or the infinite in space. The eternity of the world seizes our intelligence even more vividly than its immensity. How can a mind that refuses to attribute any bounds to the universe even bear the thought of its own non-existence? Matter did not rise out of nothingness. It shall not return to it. It is eternal, imperishable. Even though it is constantly transforming, it can neither diminish, nor increase, by one atom.[52]

If matter is infinite in time, why wouldn't it be infinite in extension too? Both infinites are inseparable. The one must imply the other; otherwise we would collapse into contradiction and absurdity. Science has not yet discovered the law of interdependence of space and the globes that travel across it. Heat, movement, light, electricity, necessarily exist throughout the whole of space. Some competent men believe that no part of the universe can be divorced from those great glowing hearths that bestow life upon the worlds. Our opuscule relies entirely upon the opinion which holds that the infinity of space is populated by an infinite number of globes and leaves no room in any corner for darkness, for solitude and for immobility.

## II. The Indefinite

Any conception of the infinite, however faint, must be borrowed from the indefinite, and even this weak idea takes on formidable appearances. Sixty-two digits, written over a length of about 15 centimeters, give 20 octodecillion leagues,[53] or in more usual terms, bil-lions of billions of billions of billions of billions of times the distance that separates the sun from the earth.

Let us now imagine a line of digits, running from here to the sun, that is to say, not of 15 centimeters, but of 37 billions of leagues. Isn't the space frightening, that such a figure represents? Now, take this figure itself as a unit in the following new number: the line of digits that describes it begins on the earth and stretches to that star, over there, whose light takes more than a thousand years to reach us, at a speed of 75,000 leagues per second. What would be the result of such a calculation, assuming that the tongue could even find enough words and time to enunciate it!

In this way, one may prolong the *indefinite* at will without transgressing the bounds of human intelligence, but also without even beginning to bite into the infinite. Let every word indicate the most frightening of distances, it would still take billions and billions of centuries, talking at one word per second, to express a distance which is only an insignificance when it comes to infinity.

## III. The Prodigious Distance of the Stars

The universe seems to unfold, immense, before our eyes. In actual fact, it only shows us a very small corner. The sun is merely one of the stars of the Milky Way, the great astral gathering that occupies half of the sky, and whose constellations are just detached, disparate sections scattered over the nightly vault. Beyond it, a few imperceptible points, pinned to the heavens, signaling the existence of stars whose glow is dimmed by distance, further still, in the faint depths, the telescope divines some nebulæ, a little bunch of whitish dust, the Milky Ways of remote confines.

The remoteness of these bodies is formidable. It eludes all the calculations of the astronomers, who have vainly tried to assign a parallax to the shiniest of them: Sirius, Altair, and Vega (the Lyre). Their results have not satisfied the public and they remain very controversial. They propose approximations, or rather a minimum, by locating the nearest star at more than 7,000 billion leagues. The better-observed one among them, the 61st of Cygnus, was assigned a distance of 23,000 billion leagues, 658,700 times the distance from the earth to the sun.[54]

Light itself, traveling at 75,000 leagues per second, reaches this distance in no less than ten years and three months. The voyage by rail, at a speed of ten leagues an hour, would take 250 millions of years without any stop or deceleration. On that same train, it would take one only 400 years to travel to the sun. The earth, which travels 233 millions of leagues every year, would not reach the 61st of Cygnus in less than one hundred thousand years.

The stars are suns similar to our own. Sirius is said to be one hundred and fifty times larger. This is possible, but largely unverifiable. Undoubtedly, such luminescent hearths must exhibit wide differences in volume. Yet, any comparison is out of the question, and the differences in size and brilliance can only trigger questions of distance or rather trigger skepticism. Indeed, without sufficient data, any assessment is recklessness.

## IV. The Physical Composition of the Stars

Nature's art of adapting organisms to their milieus without straying from its general overarching plan is marvelous. It is only by using simple modifications that it multiplies the types in impossible measures. It has been wrongly supposed that the celestial bodies were home to equally fantastical situations and beings, having no resemblance to the inhabitants of our planet. The fact that myriads of forms and mechanisms do exist is beyond doubt. But the plan and the materials are invariable. One is entitled to affirm without any hesitation that even at the extremities of the universe, the basis of all animal existence lies in the nervous centers, and that electricity is its principal agent. All other equipment is subordinate to this one, across thousands of incarnations determined by the milieu. Such is undoubtedly the case in our planetary group, which must exhibit an innumerable series of various assemblages. One does not even need to leave the earth to see such a nearly limitless diversity.

We have always considered our globe to be the queen of all planets; our vanity has often been humiliated. We're almost mere intruders in the very group that our arrogance intends to subject to its supremacy. It is density that determines the physical constitution of a star. However, our density is not that of the solar system. It is in fact a rare exception that nearly throws us outside of the true family, made of the sun and the big planets. In the whole of the procession, the volume of Mercury, Venus, the Earth and Mars together accounts for 2 out of 2,417, make it 2 out of 1,281,684 with the sun thrown in. We might as well count for zero!

Only a few years ago, such a contrast kept wide open the realm of fantastical speculation over the structure of the celestial bodies. The only thing that no one deemed doubtful was that they should not resemble our planet in any way. We were mistaken. Spectral analysis allowed us to dissipate this mistake, and demonstrate, in spite of strong evidence to the contrary, that the composition of the universe was unified. The forms are innumerable, but the elements are the same. Here we come to the fundamental question, a question that soars high above all others and dwarfs them; we must therefore explore it in detail by moving from the known to the unknown.

Until further notice, on our globe nature has at its disposal the 64 *simple bodies* named below. We say "until further notice" because the number of such bodies was only 53 a few years ago. Every now and again, their nomenclature gets enriched with the discovery of some metal, painstakingly extracted by chemistry from the stubborn bonds that link them to oxygen. In all likelihood, the 64 will reach the 100. But the serious agents are hardly more than 25. The rest share the bill only as stooges. They are called *simple bodies*, because hitherto, they have been found to be irreducible. We are arranging them more or less in order of importance:

1. Hydrogen
2. Oxygen
3. Nitrogen
4. Carbon
5. Phosphorus
6. Sulfur
7. Calcium
8. Silicon
9. Potassium
10. Sodium
11. Aluminum
12. Chlorine
13. Iodine
14. Iron
15. Magnesium
16. Copper
17. Silver
18. Lead
19. Mercury
20. Antimony
21. Barium
22. Chromium
23. Bromine
24. Bismuth
25. Zinc
26. Arsenic
27. Platinum
28. Tin
29. Gold
30. Nickel
31. Beryllium
32. Fluorine

33. Manganese
34. Zirconium
35. Cobalt
36. Iridium
37. Boron
38. Strontium
39. Molybdenum
40. Palladium
41. Titanium
42. Cadmium
43. Selenium
44. Osmium
45. Rubidium
46. Lanthanum
47. Tellurium
48. Tungsten
49. Uranium
50. Tantalum
51. Lithium
52. Niobium
53. Rhodium
54. Didymiumi[55]
55. Indium
56. Terbium
57. Thallium
58. Thorium
59. Vanadium
60. Yttrium
61. Caesium
62. Ruthenium
63. Erbium
64. Cerium

The first four, hydrogen, oxygen, nitrogen, and carbon, are the great agents of nature. We do not know which of these to give precedence to since their action is so universal. Hydrogen is first, because it is the light of all suns. Those four gases alone constitute nearly all organic matter, flora and fauna, with the adjunction of calcium, phosphorus, sulfur, sodium, potassium, etc.

Hydrogen and oxygen form water, with the adjunction of chlorine, sodium, and iodine for the seas. Silicon, calcium, aluminum and magnesium, in combination with oxygen, carbon, etc., compose the great masses of geological terrains and the superposed layers of the terrestrial crust. As regards precious metals, they have more importance for humans than for nature.

Till recently, those elements were held to be specific to our globe. What debates took place about the sun for example, about its composition, the origin and the nature of its light! The great controversy opposing *emission* and *waves* is now only just settled. Only its last rear-guard gunshots are still being heard.[56] The victorious *waves* had built a rather fantastical theory upon their success: "The sun, a simple and opaque body just like any other planet, is enveloped in two atmospheres, the one, which resembles ours, serves as an umbrella that protects the indigenous peoples against the second, called photosphere, which is the eternal and inexhaustible source of light and heat."

This widely accepted doctrine has long reigned over science, in spite of all the analogies it contradicts. The central fire that hisses below our feet suffices to confirm that our earth once was what our sun is today, and the earth was never covered with any perennial and electrical photosphere.

Spectral analysis has dissipated such errors.[57] It is no longer a question of inexhaustible and perpetual electricity, but more prosaically it is a matter of hydrogen burning, here like there, in conjunction with oxygen. The pink protuberances are formidable spurts of flaming gas, which exceed the disc of the moon during total solar eclipses. As regards the sunspots, one was right to conceive of them as large funnels opening into gaseous masses. It is the hydrogen flame, swept by storms over immense surfaces, and offering a glimpse of the core of the star, be it in a liquid or in a greatly compressed gaseous state, not as a dark opacity, but rather as a relative obscurity.

So, no more chimeras. Here we see two terrestrial elements providing light to the universe, just like they provide light to the streets of Paris and London. It is their combination that spreads light and heat. It is the product of this combination, water, which creates and entertains organic life. No water, no atmosphere, no flora or fauna. Nothing but the cadaver of the moon.

Ocean of flames in the stars for enlivening, ocean of water on the planets for organizing, the association of hydrogen and oxygen is the government of matter, and sodium is their inseparable companion in both of their two opposed forms, fire and water. In the solar spectrum, this combination shines brighter than any other; it is the principal element of the salt of the seas.

Although so peaceful nowadays in spite of some slight wrinkles, those seas have known whole other types of storms in the past, when they whirled into devouring flames on the lavas of our globe. It is nonetheless the very same mass of hydrogen and oxygen now as it was then, but what a metamorphosis! Evolution is accomplished. It shall be accomplished on the sun just as well. Its spots already indicate the existence of temporary lacunæ in the combustion of hydrogen, and time will only increase and multiply such lapses until they become permanent. This will take centuries to happen, no doubt, but the decrease has begun.

The sun is a declining star. One day will come when the combination of hydrogen and oxygen, no longer able to decompose itself in order to re-create the two elements separately, will remain what it ought to be: water. On that day, the reign of the flames shall be brought to an end and that of aqueous vapors, whose last word is the sea, shall begin. Once these vapors envelop the fallen star with their thick masses, our planetary world shall fall into eternal night.

Before this fateful end, humanity will have the time to learn a number of things. It already knows, thanks to *spectrometry*, that half of the 64 *simple bodies* that compose our planet also exist in the sun, the stars, and their entourage. Mankind knows that the whole universe draws light, heat, and organic life from the association of hydrogen and oxygen, as flames or water.

Not all of the *simple bodies* appear in the solar spectrum, and conversely, the spectrums of the sun and the stars reveal the existence of elements unknown to us. But this science is still new and inexperienced. It is barely uttering its first words and they are decisive. The elements that compose the celestial bodies are identical everywhere. Every tomorrow shall only unfold further the evidence of such an identity. At first, it seemed that the discrepancies in density were an insurmountable obstacle to any similarity between the planets of our system, but they are now losing much of their isolating significance, as we see that the sun, whose density is a mere quarter of ours, contains metals such as iron (density 7.80), nickel (8.67), copper (9.95), zinc (7.19), cobalt (7.81), cadmium (8.69), chromium (5.90).

Nothing is more natural than the fact that *simple bodies* exist on a variety of globes in different proportions, causing discrepancies in density. Granted, the materials of a nebula must find their respective place on the surface of the planets according to the laws of gravity, but this arrangement does not prevent the *simple bodies* from coexisting within the whole of the nebula and then to order themselves in accordance to these laws. It is precisely the case in our system, and, as it appears, in the other stellar groups too. We shall turn to the consequences of this fact in a moment.

## V. Observations on Laplace's Cosmogony—The Comets

Laplace[58] took his system from Herschel,[59] who took it from his telescope. A mathematician through and through, the illustrious geometer devotes a lot of time to the movements of the stars and little time to their nature. He grants attention to the physical question only nonchalantly, content with giving simple affirmations, in his haste to return to his constant concern for gravitational calculations. Clearly, his theory is at grips with two fundamental challenges: the origin of the nebulæ and their high temperature on the one hand, and the comets on the other. Let us delay our discussion of the nebulæ and look at the comets. As he had no way to accommodate them into his system, the author resolved to get rid of them by sending them bouncing from star to star. Let us track them down, so as to get rid of them ourselves.

Nowadays everyone has come to deeply despise those comets as miserable toys to the superior planets that rough them up, tear them apart in hundreds of ways, inflate them with solar fires, and finally throw them away in tatters. Complete degeneration! How humble was our former respect, when they were greeted as messengers of death! How many boos and whistles now that we know them to be harmless! There is mankind for us.

Still, our impertinence is not without a slight nuance of anxiety. Oracles do not shy from contradiction. Hence, after having affirmed the nullity of the comets dozens of times, after having assured us that the most perfect vacuum of some pneumatic machine was far denser than comet matter, Arago still claims, in a chapter of his works, that "the transformation of the earth into the satellite of some comet is an event that does not fall outside of the range of probabilities."[60]

Such a grave and serious scholar as Laplace also professes both the pros and the cons on this question. He says at one point: "The encounter of the earth with a comet cannot produce any noticeable effect. It is highly likely that comets *have enveloped it several times without having been noticed*..."[61] And elsewhere: "It is easy to imagine the effects of this collision [of a comet] on the earth: the axis and the circular motion change; the seas abandoning their ancient position to rush towards a new equator; a great number of men and animals drowned in this universal deluge, or destroyed in the violent shock inflicted to the globe, entire species annihilated..."[62] etc.

Such adamant *yes* and *no* are unusual in the writings of mathematicians. The law of attraction, the fundamental dogma of astronomy, is sometimes equally mistreated. This is what we shall see by saying a word about zodiacal light.

This phenomenon has already received different explanations. It was first attributed to the atmosphere of the sun, against Laplace. According to him, "the solar atmosphere does not reach half way to the orb of Mercury. Zodiacal glows are caused by molecules too volatile to have attached themselves to the planets, at the time of the great primal formation, and nowadays they circulate around a core star. Their extreme slightness does not oppose any resistance to the workings of any celestial body, and gives us this clarity that is permeable to the stars."[63]

Such a hypothesis is unlikely. Planetary molecules made volatile under the effect of high temperature do not maintain their heat forever, and therefore, neither do they sustain their gaseous form in the icy deserts of space. What is more, and with all due respect to Laplace, this matter, however slight one makes it out to be, would represent a serious obstacle to the movement of the celestial bodies, and would cause great disorder in time.

The same objection applies to the recent idea that attributes to zodiacal lights the honor of being the remains of wrecked comets, wandering through the storms of the perihelia. According to this view, such fragments would form a vast ocean, encompassing and even exceeding the orbits of Mercury, Venus, and the Earth. Conflating in this way the nullity of the comets with that of the ether or perhaps even of a vacuum is pushing one's disregard for the comets a little far. No, the planets would not enjoy a pleasant journey going through such nebulosity, and gravitation would not take long to find itself mistreated there too.

It seems even less rational to seek the origin of the mysterious glows of the zodiacal region in some ring of meteorites presumably circulating around the sun. By nature, meteorites are not very permeable to the light of the stars.

Perhaps we may find a path towards the truth by walking back some of the way. Arago said—I have forgotten where: "it has frequently been possible for comet matter to enter our atmosphere. This event is without danger. We may, without even noticing it, travel across the tail of a comet..."[64] Laplace is no less explicit: "It is highly probable," he writes, "that comets have enveloped the earth several times without having been noticed..."[65]

Everyone would agree with this. But one is entitled to ask the two astronomers what has become of these comets. Have they pursued their voyage? Are they able to free themselves from the embrace of the earth and to pass it by? Must the law of attraction be confiscated? What! This vague comet-exuded scent, whose nothingness makes tired the tongue that seeks to define it, would challenge the force that rules the universe!

One may grant that two massive globes, thrown with full force, may cross each other tangentially and continue on their course after a double tremor. But to affirm that some wandering inanities would come and stick themselves against our atmosphere, before peacefully detaching themselves and following their path, this is unacceptable boldness. Why don't these diffuse vapors remain nailed to our earth by gravity?

"Precisely," one might say, "it is that they weigh nothing. It is their insubstantiality itself that subtracts them to the general rule. No mass, no attraction." This reasoning is mistaken. If they part from us in order to join their army corps, it is because the army corps attracts them and pulls them away. In what capacity? The earth's power is far superior. The comets, as we know, do not disturb anyone, but everyone disturbs them, because they are the humble slaves of attraction. How could they ever stop obeying even as our globe robustly takes them away and should never let go of their grasp? The sun is too remote to have any intention of taking them away from whoever holds them so near, and should it drag away the head of such a crowd, the rear guard, broken off and dislocated, would still remain within the powers of the earth.

All the same, astronomers are talking of comets surrounding and then abandoning our globe as if it were something really quite simple. No one has made any observation in this regard. Is the swift motion of the stars really sufficient to extract them from the earth's influence, and let them pursue their course on the acquired impetus?

Such an attack on the law of gravity is impossible and it seems to indicate that we are on the tail of zodiacal glows. The comet's detachments, once trapped in such heavenly encounters and ejected back towards the equator by the rotation of the earth, end up forming lenticular swellings, which light up under sunbeams, right before dawn and especially after dusk. The heat of the day has dilated them and made their luminosity more noticeable than it is in the mornings, after the cooling of the night.

These diaphanous masses, with their comet-like appearance, are permeable to the smallest of stars, occupying immeasurable expanses from the equator at their center, where their altitude and shine are greatest, to the remotes that lay far beyond the tropics, and probably stretch all the way to both poles, where they decline, contract, and extinguish themselves.

Until now, it was always assumed that the zodiacal light lay outside the earth, and it was difficult to assign it a place and to decide upon its nature so as to reconcile both its permanence and its variations. But it is in the earth itself that the cause of it lies, as it is wrapped around its own atmosphere, and as the weight of the atmospheric column does not increase by a single atom. This is the most decisive proof of the inanity of this poor substance.

It may be that the visits of the comets renew the imprisoned contingents more often than we think. Such contingents, however, are unable to exceed a certain height without being taken away by a centrifugal force pulling its bounty into outer space. The terrestrial atmosphere is therefore doubled out with a comet-like envelope, more or less immeasurable, the seat and the source of zodiacal light. This hypothesis fits well with the diaphanous nature of the comets, and moreover, it takes stock of the laws of gravity, which prevent the loose elements captured by the planets from escaping.

Let us return to the history of these hairy nihilities. Their avoiding Saturn only throws them into the arms of Jupiter, the policeman of this system. Ambushed in the shade, it smells the comets even before any sunbeam makes them visible, and it leads them, panicked, into the perilous abysses. There, abandoned to the hands of heat and dilated to the point of monstrosity, they loose their form, become elongated, dissolve and rush through the dreadful pass, shedding slowpokes everywhere before painstakingly recovering their unknown solitudes, under the protection of the cold.

Those comets alone make it through that escaped the trappings of the planetary zone. Therefore, avoiding fateful passes, and eluding the big spiders of the zodiacal plains that linger around their webs, the comet of 1811 washes over the ecliptic, from the polar heights spilling out over the sun, and promptly circling it before regrouping and reforming its immense columns once scattered under enemy fire. Only then, after the maneuver has succeeded, does it parade before our amazed eyes with the splendor of its army, before majestically continuing its victorious retreat towards deep space.

Such triumphs are rare. The poor comets come, by the thousands, to burn themselves at the candle. Just like moths, they rush in lightly, from the deep of the night, to waltz around the flame that draws them in, but they do not escape without strewing the fields of the ecliptic with their wrecked carcasses. There lies, according to some observers of the heavens, a vast comet cemetery that spreads from the sun to beyond the terrestrial orb and whose mysterious glows are visible on the evenings and mornings of pure days. The dead ones are recognizable by these ghostly gleams in which the living lights of the stars reflect themselves.

On the contrary, we must ask, are they not supplicating prisoners, chained for centuries to the barriers of our atmosphere, and begging in vain for freedom and hospitality? From its first ray to its last, the inter-tropical sun shows us those pale Gypsies, expiating so painfully their indiscreet visits to well-established people.

Comets are truly fantastic beings. Since the solar system was established, millions of them have passed within the pericentral distance of the earth. Our particular world is replete with them, and yet, more than half of them elude our vision, and even our telescopes. How many of those nomads have chosen our place as their home?... Three..., and still it could be said that they merely live under a tent. One of these days, they will up and leave to join the innumerable tribes that dwell in the imaginary expanses. It is of little importance, in truth, that this be achieved by way of ellipses, parabolas, or hyperbolas.

After all, they are harmless and graceful creatures that often hold the lead role in the most beautiful of starry nights. If it is true that they foolishly rush into the trap, astronomy is caught along with them and finds itself even worse for it than they. They are true scientific nightmares. What contrast with celestial bodies! They are two extreme opposites, the crushing masses and the weightless things, the excess of the gigantic and the excess of nothingness.

And yet, Laplace describes this nothingness in terms of condensation and vaporization, as if it were just any old gas. He affirms that in time, the pericentral heats entirely dissolve the comets into space. What becomes of them once volatilized? The author doesn't say and he probably doesn't mind too much. As soon as it is no longer a matter of geometry, he proceeds roughly, and without much scruple. Yet, however ethereal the sublimation of the hairy stars may be, it is still material. What shall be its destiny? Undoubtedly, it shall later recover its primitive form under the action of the cold. That may be. In this case, some essence of comet produces ambulatory diaphaneities. But, according to Laplace and other authors, such diaphaneities are nothing other than fixed nebulæ.

Hey! My oh my! Halt! We must stop the words in their course and verify their content. *Nebula* is suspect. It is a name far too well deserved; indeed, it has three different meanings. It designates: 1) a whitish glow, which strong telescopes decompose into innumerable little stars clustered tightly together; 2) a pale light, of similar appearance, pinned with one or several little brilliant points, but which doesn't let itself be broken up into stars; and 3) the comets.

It is indispensable to carefully handle all three of these individual things separately. The first one—the cluster of little stars—poses no difficulty. It is agreed. The debate applies only to the other two. According to Laplace, when undergoing a first degree of condensation, nebulosities, spread generously across the uni- verse, create either comets or some nebulæ made of brilliant points irreducible to stars. They later transform into solar systems. Laplace explains and describes this transformation in great detail.

As regards the comets however, he satisfies himself with representing them as little, undefined, and wandering nebulosities, which he makes no effort to distinguish from those nebulæ pregnant with stellar children. On the contrary, he stresses their close resemblance, preventing anyone from drawing a distinction between them based on anything other than the difference in the way the comets appear to move when they are caught by the rays of the sun. In a word, he finds the irreducible nebulæ in Herschel's telescope and attributes them to the comets and to the planetary systems alike. To him, everything comes down to a question of orbits and of fixed or irregular gravitation. For Laplace in any case, "the nebulæ scattered across the universe" all have the same origin and therefore the same constitution.[66]

How can such a great physicist identify lights that are icy, borrowed, and empty with the huge jets of ardent vapors that will someday become suns? If at least the comets were made of hydrogen, this would be acceptable. Then one would be allowed to suppose that great masses of this gas, remaining outside the star-nebulæ, wander freely across the expanse where they perform the little drama of gravitation. Yet this would be assuming that the gas is cold and obscure, whereas the stello-planetary cradles are in fact incandescent, so that the assimilation between these two sorts of nebulæ would still be impossible. But even this tactic fails. Compared to the comets, hydrogen is granite. The nebulous matter of stellar systems cannot have anything in common with that of comets. One is force, light, weight and heat; the other, nothingness, ice, void and darkness.

Laplace talks about a similitude so perfect between the two kinds of nebulæ that one is at pains to distinguish between them. What! Volatile nebulæ lie at an immeasurable distance, while the comets are almost within hand's reach, and we should conclude from a false resemblance between two bodies separated by such an abyss that they possess the same constitution! But a comet is infinitely small, and the nebula is almost a universe. Any comparison between such facts is an aberration.

Let us repeat that if it were possible that during the volatile state of the nebulæ, part of its hydrogen eluded both attraction and combustion and thereby set itself free in space to become a comet, then such stars would therefore enter the general constitution of the universe. Such stars, besides, could play an important role. As a mass, they would be powerless, but once inflamed by the shock with the air and the contact with oxygen, they would burn to death all organized bodies, plants, and animals. However, everyone agrees that hydrogen is to the comet-like substance what a block of marble would be to hydrogen itself.

Let us now suppose that tatters of stellar nebulæ are indeed floating around like comets from one system to the other. Such volatile clusters, taken to a maximum temperature, would appear to us not as a subtle, immobile, and unassuming fog, but rather like the dreadful jet of light and heat required to finally bring our polemics about them to an end. Uncertainty about comets has been going on for ages. Discussions and conjectures achieve nothing. Yet, a few points seem to be clearer now. For example, the unity of the comet-like substance is now beyond doubt. It is a simple body, whose apparitions have never exhibited any variation, and there have already been many. We constantly observe the same expendable fragility which dilatation goes to the confines of emptiness, as well as this absolute transparency, which does not hinder the course of even the smallest lights.

Comets are neither ether, nor gas, nor liquid, nor solid, nor in any way akin to any of the substances found in the celestial bodies, but they are made of an indefinable substance, which appears to have none of the properties of known matter and does not exist outside of the sunbeams, which draw them out of nothingness for a minute, before returning them to it. Between the sidereal enigma that is a comet and the stellar systems that constitute the universe, there is a radical separation. They are two isolated modes of existence, two fully distinct categories of matter with no other link than the disorderly action of a near-insane gravity. There is no reason to include the comets in a description of the world. They are nothing, they do nothing, and their only role is that of an enigma.

With its excessive pericentral dilatation, and its icy apocentral contractions, this loony star is like some giant from the Arabian Nights, bottled up by Solomon, and occasionally venturing little by little out of its prison, to regain human form, before being vaporized again and sucked back into the neck of the bottle, at whose bottom it disappears again. A comet: it's an ounce of fog that covers a billion cubic-leagues, then fills a carafe.

Enough with these toys, they make no contribution to solving the key question: "Are all nebulæ a cluster of adult stars, or must we admit that some of them are star fetuses, be they single or multiple?" Only two judges can answer this question: the telescope and spectral analysis. Let us demand from them the strict impartiality that eludes the occult influence of the great names. It seems, in fact, that spectrometry is gradually inclined to find results that concur with Laplace's theory.

Any lenience before the possible errors of the illustrious mathematician would be all the more pointless that by drawing from the contemporary knowledge of the solar system, his theory gathers a force sufficient to outweigh even the telescope and spectral analysis, which says a lot. It is the only rational and reasonable explanation for planetary mechanics, and it would surely yield under only the most irrefutable of arguments...

## VI. Origin of the Worlds

There is a weak point to this theory however... The same as always, the question of the origin, which Laplace dodges this time by avoidance. Unfortunately, eluding is not solving. Laplace cleverly turned this difficulty around by leaving it for others to solve. As far as he is concerned, he worked out his own hypothesis, and sent it on its way, free of this stumbling block.

Gravity only goes halfway toward explaining the universe. The motion of celestial bodies obeys two forces: centripetal force or gravity, which makes them fall or attracts them to each other, and centrifugal force, which pushes them forward in a straight line. These two forces combined result in the more or less elliptic motion of all the celestial bodies. Remove the centrifugal force, the earth falls into the sun. Remove the centripetal force, it turns its orbit loose, follows its tangent, and forges straight ahead.[67]

We know the source of centripetal force: it is attraction, or gravitation. The origin of centrifugal force remains a mystery. Laplace left that obstacle aside. In his theory, the movement of translation, that is to say, centrifugal force, originates in the rotation of the nebula. This hypothesis is true, without a doubt, since one could not give a more suitable account of the phenomena that take place in our planetary group. However, one is entitled to ask the illustrious geometer: "Where does this rotation of the nebula come from? Where does the heat responsible for volatilizing this gigantic mass which will later become condensed into a sun and its surrounding planets come from?"

Heat! One would think all we need to do is to bend down and pick it up in space. Yes, if what we want is heat that is 270 degrees below zero. Does Laplace mean this sort of heat when he writes that *due to excessive heat, the atmosphere of the sun stretched primarily beyond the orbs of all planets*?[68] He acknowledges, after Herschel, the existence of a great number of nebulosities, at first so diffuse that they are barely visible, before attaining to the status of stars as a result of a series of condensations. Yet, these stars are gigantic incandescent globes like the sun and this indicates a considerable degree of heat. What must have been their temperature when, still in their vaporous state, such enormous masses became dilated to such a degree of volatilization that all we could see of them was a barely perceptible nebulosity!

According to Laplace, those very nebulosities are the ones that are spread profusely across the universe, giving birth to comets and solar systems. This assertion is inacceptable, as we demonstrated with regard to the comet-like substance which, as we showed, can have nothing in common with the substance of nebulous stars. Assuming these substances were similar, it would follow that the comets are always and everywhere mixed with stellar matter. Thus, they would share their existence and would not constantly follow their own path and behave like strangers to all stars through their inconsistent motions, their wandering habits, and the absolute unity of substance that characterizes them.

Laplace is perfectly right to say: "Thus, the progress of the condensation of nebulous matter leads us to view the sun as having been formerly surrounded with a vast atmosphere. We obtain this view, as was shown, thanks to an examination of the phenomena of the solar system. Such a remarkable encounter bestows a nearly certain degree of likelihood to this characterization of the former state of the sun."[69] However, nothing is more mistaken than to conflate the comets—those icy weightless inertias—with the stellar nebulæ that represent the massive parts of nature and are supported by the *maximum* volatilization of temperature and light. There is no doubt that the comets remain a frustrating enigma because, insofar as they remain inexplicable when everything else is, they become a nearly insurmountable obstacle to our knowledge of the universe. But one never triumphs over an obstacle by replacing it with an absurdity. Better to concede a defeat and attribute to such impalpabilities some special sort of existence outside of matter strictly defined. This existence must be conceived as capable of acting upon matter through gravity, but without being subject to its influence. Although they are fleeting, unstable, and short-lived, we know them to be made of a single, invariable, and simple substance, incapable of modification. Comets are liable to divide themselves, to regroup, to form masses or to tear themselves into tatters, never to change. Therefore, they do not take part in the perpetual becoming of nature. Let us find comfort from this logogriph in reminding ourselves of its inconsequentiality.

The question of origins is much more serious. Laplace sold it short, or rather he did not take any notice of it, and did not even bring himself to talk about it. With the help of his telescope, Herschel recorded a great number of clusters of nebulous matter in space, with different degrees of diffusion. Through progressive cooling these clusters finally turn into stars. The illustrious geometer explains these transformations and tells their story very well, but he doesn't say a word about the origins of these nebulosities. Naturally, one may ask oneself: "Where do these nebulæ come from, with their ability to turn into planets and suns, under the action of relative coolness?"

According to some theories, there is chaotic matter in the extension. This matter would have the property to cluster together and form planetary nebulæ under the action of heat and attraction. Why, and since when, must we assume the existence of such chaotic matter? Whence does this extraordinary heat come from, that comes to facilitate the task? These are questions no one asks, sparing themselves the effort of answering them.

It is vain to say that chaotic matter, which constitutes the modern planets, also constituted the ancient ones, implying that the universe is no older than the oldest planets present today. We willingly grant immeasurable age to these stars, but we know nothing of their beginnings except for the original agglomeration of chaotic matter and of their end, silence. The pleasantry that all these theories make is to establish a factory producing heat at will, lying there, in the imaginary expanses, providing indefinite volatilization power for every nebula and every chaotic matter one may think up.

Laplace, the scrupulous geometer, is a slack physicist. He vaporizes all over the place, *by virtue of excessive heat*. Once one accepts Laplace's condensing nebulæ, one admiringly follows him down his description of the successive birth of planets and of their satellites, through gradual cooling. But this unborn nebulous matter, pulled in every direction, without anyone knowing how or why, also has a remarkable cooling effect on our enthusiasm. It is less than decent to sit one's reader on a hypothesis supported by nothing, and to dump him there.

Heat and light do not build up in space, they dissipate. Their source is exhaustible. All celestial bodies cool down as they radiate. The stars, which began as formidable blazes, end in a dark freeze. Once, our seas were an ocean of flames. Now they are nothing but water. When the sun extinguishes itself, they shall become a block of ice. Let the cosmogonies that dream up the world of yesterday believe that the stars are only burning their first tank. After? These millions of stars, the illumination of our nights, their days are numbered. They began in a bonfire, they will end in the cold and the night.

Is it enough to say: this will always last longer than ourselves? Let us take it. *Carpe diem*. What do we care for what used to be? What do we care for what shall be? "*Avant et après nous le déluge*!"[70] No, the enigma of the universe is constantly before our every thought. The human spirit wants to decipher it at all costs. Laplace was on the right track when he wrote: "Seen from the sun, the moon seems to travel in epicycloids, whose centers lay on the circumference of the earth's orbit. Similarly, the earth describes a series of epicycloids, whose centers lay on the curve followed by the sun around the center of gravity of the group of stars that he belongs to. Finally, the sun itself follows a series of epicycloids whose centers are on the curve followed by the center of gravity of this group around that of the universe."[71]

"*Of the universe!*" this is saying a lot. This so-called center of the universe, with the immense procession gravitating around it, is nothing but an imperceptible dot in the expanse. Still, Laplace was truly on the track of the truth, and he almost touched upon the key to the enigma. Only, this phrase: "*of the universe*," is proof that he touched it without seeing it, or at least, without looking at it. He was an ultra-mathematician. Down to the marrow of his bones, he believed in a harmony and an unchangeable solidity of the celestial mechanics. Solid, very solid, indeed. Yet one must make a distinction between the universe and a clock.

When a clock slows down, it is readjusted. When it is damaged, it is fixed. When it is used, it is replaced. But who repairs and renovates celestial bodies? Do such flaming globes, however splendidly they represent matter, enjoy eternal youth? No, matter is eternal only in its elements or as a whole. All of its forms—humble and sublime alike—are transitory and perishable. Stars are born, shine, die out, and even as they survive their lost splendor for thousands of centuries, all they offer to the laws of gravity are wandering tombs. How many billions of icy cadavers are crawling like this in the night of space, awaiting the hour of destruction, which will be, at the same time, the hour of resurrection!

Indeed, the departed of matter always return to life, whatever their condition. If the night of the tomb is long for the mortal stars, there comes a moment when their flame lights up again like lightning. On the surface of the planets, under the rays of the sun, the form dies out and quickly degrades to return its elements to a new form. Metamorphoses take place again and again without interruption. But once a frozen sun dies out, who will be there to give it back its heat and light? It can only return to life as a sun. It bestowed specks of life to a myriad of diverse beings. It can only pass it on to its sons through marriage. How must we conceive of the matrimony and of the fathering of such giants of light?

Once one of these immeasurable whirls of stars, having been born, gravitated and died at the term millions of centuries, it completes its wandering across the regions of space that lay open before it. Then, its outer frontiers collide with other extinguished whirls coming its way. A furious melee rages for countless years, on a battlefield billions of billions of leagues wide. In this part of the universe, all is now nothing more than a vast atmosphere of flames, ceaselessly stabbed by the volatilized lightning of conflagrations that annihilate stars and planets in the blink of an eye.

Not for a moment does this pandemonium depart from its obedience to the laws of nature. A succession of shocks vaporizes the solid masses that immediately fall into the grasp of gravitation, which then gathers them into nebulæ sent spinning by the shock, and assigns them a regular course around the new centers. Then, through the lens of their telescopes, remote observers watch the stage of these great revolutions; they see a pale light, mixed with more luminous points. The light is but a stain, but this stain is an entire nation of resuscitating globes.

Every one of these newborns shall first have a lonely childhood, as a fiery and turbulent cloud.

Having become calmer with time, the young star will gradually draw from its own bosom a large family, soon cooled down by isolation and now only subsisting thanks to the paternal warmth. He shall be the only representative of his dynasty in a world that will know only him, and he will never lay eyes on his children. Here is our planetary system, and we inhabit one of its youngest daughters, senior to only one sister, Venus, and one young brother, Mercury, the last one to have hatched.

Is it truly thus that worlds are reborn? I do not know. Maybe the dead legions clashing in a bid to regain life are less numerous, maybe the field of resurrection is less vast. But certainly, it is only a question of number and extension, not of means. No one is entitled to decide whether the encounter takes place simply between two stellar groups, between two systems where every star, along with its procession, is not yet playing the role of a planet, or between two centers where it is now nothing more than a satellite, or finally between two matrixes that represent a corner of the universe. The only legitimate certainty is this:

Matter cannot diminish or increase by one atom. The stars are only short-lived torches. So, once they are extinguished, and unless they light up again, night and death are bound to take over the universe in time. So, how could they light up again if not thanks to motion transformed into heat in huge proportions, that is to say, thanks to a collision that volatilizes them and summons them to a new existence? Let's not object that the transformation of motion into heat would annihilate motion, and that the globes would be immobilized. Motion is only the result of attraction, and attraction is inexhaustible, being a permanent property of all bodies. Motion suddenly reappears out of the shock itself, in new directions perhaps, but always resulting from the same cause: gravity.

Do you object that such violent changes jeopardize the laws of gravitation? You have no idea of it, nor do I. Our unique resource is in consulting Analogy. Here's what she says: "For centuries, meteorites fall in the millions on our globe, and doubtless, on the planets of every stellar system. It is a grave breach of the law of attraction, in your sense of the word. In fact, it is a form of attraction that you ignore, or rather, that you overlook, because it applies to asteroids, and not to the stars. After gravitating for millions of years, according to the rules, they have suddenly penetrated the atmosphere, violating the rule, and there they transformed motion into heat, by way of their fusion, or of their volatilization, or of the air friction. What happens to the little people may and must happen to the greats too. Let us produce gravitation before the tribunal of the *Observatoire*, try her for having maliciously and illegitimately thrown or dropped on the earth the æroliths that were entrusted to her and which she was to keep spinning in the vacuum."

Yes, gravitation dropped them, is dropping them now, and will drop them in the future, just like it has hit the old planets, as it is hitting them now, and as it will hit the old stars in the future. As they are wandering in an old cemetery, the departed, being hit by gravity, are now exploding like fireworks, and torches are now glimmering and lighting up the world. If the means do not suit you, find a better one. But be careful. Stars only last a while and, combined with their planets, they represent the whole of matter. If you do not resurrect them, the universe is finite. Anyway, we shall pursue our demonstration on every mode, major and minor, with- out fearing repetition. The topic is worth the effort. Whether we know or ignore how the universe subsists is not a matter of indifference.

Thus, until further notice, we shall affirm that stars die of old age, and that they are reborn in a shock. Such is the way that sidereal entities transform matter. What other process would allow them to obey the laws of change while escaping eternal immobilization? Laplace says: "There exist obscure bodies in outer space, as considerable, and perhaps just as numerous, as the stars."[72] These bodies are nothing but dead stars. Are they condemned to a cadaverous perpetuity? Will all the living ones, without exception, join them forever? How can these vacancies be filled?

The origin that Laplace assigns—very vaguely—to stellar nebulæ, is unlikely. They are, according to him, a cluster of nebulosities, of volatilized cosmic clouds, an incessant aggregation formed shortly in space. But how? Everywhere space is how we see it, cold and dark. Stellar systems are enormous masses of matter: where do they come from? The vacuum? To improvise such nebulosities is not acceptable.

And as regards the idea of chaotic matter, it should never have re-emerged in the nineteenth century. There never was and there never shall be any shadow of chaos anywhere. The organization of the universe is eternal. It never varied by the breadth of a hair, neither did it falter, even for a second. There is no chaos, not even on those battlefields where billions of stars turn the dead into the living by colliding and setting themselves ablaze for centuries at a time. The law of attraction oversees such radical transformations just as rigorously as it governs the quietest motions of the moon.

Such cataclysms are rare in all districts of the universe, since the number of births cannot exceed the number of deaths in the registry of the infinite, and since its inhabitants enjoy an enviable longevity. The expanse that unfolds freely ahead is more than sufficient for their lifespan, and the time to die comes up much before the end of the journey. The infinite is poor neither in time nor in space. It allocates them generously and fairly between its peoples. We ignore how much time is granted, but we can get some idea of space by considering the distance that separates us from the stars, our neighbors.

The minimum interval separating us from them is ten thousand billions of leagues: an abysm. Isn't that a magnificent path, and spacious enough for a safe hike? Our sun's back is covered. Its sphere of action must probably extend to the nearest attractions. Not one area is indifferent to gravity. Here, the data fail us. We know our surroundings. In the same way, it would be interesting to determine those sources of light whose spheres of attraction confine to ours, and to organize them around it, just like one locks up a cannon ball with other cannonballs. In this way, our domain in the universe would be mapped out. Such a thing is impossible; otherwise it would have been achieved already. Unfortunately, no one will ride Jupiter or Saturn into outer space in order to measure parallaxes.

Our sun is in motion; this is made obvious by its rotation. It travels along thousands, perhaps millions of stars that surround us and belong to our army. It has been traveling for centuries, and we ignore its past, present, and future course. The historical period of mankind is already of six thousand years. As early as those times, observations of the sky were carried out in Egypt. Apart from a displacement of the zodiacal constellations, caused by the precession of equinoxes, no change in the sidereal appearance has been recorded. In six thousand years, it could have been expected that our system had had enough time to move in any direction.

For a poor hiker like our globe, six thousand years is a fifth of the distance to Sirius. Not a clue, nothing. That we came closer to the constellation of Hercules remains a mere hypothesis. We are stuck into place, and so are the stars. And yet, we are, like them, on our way towards the same goal. They are our contemporaries, our travel companions, and hence probably, their apparent immobility: we are forging ahead together. The way will be long and the time too, until we reach old age, death, and finally, resurrections. But this time and this path are a tiny dot, not even a thousandth of a second, in comparison to the infinite. Eternity makes no distinction between the star-like and the ephemeral. What are those billions of suns that succeed each other throughout time and space? A deluge of sparkles. This rain fertilizes the universe.

This is why at every minute the shock and the volatilization of the perished stars build the worlds anew in the vast fields of the infinite. Such gigantic conflagrations are both innumerable and rare, depending on whether we consider the universe or only one if its regions. In what other way could one explain how general life maintains itself? Comet-nebulæ are ghosts, stellar-nebulæ, made up of this and that, are mere chimeras. In the expanse, there is nothing but the celestial bodies, small and big, children, adults or dead, and their whole existence is up to date. As children, they are volatilized nebulæ; as adults, they are the stars and their planets; dead, they are their gloomy cadavers.

Heat, light, and motion are the forces of matter, and not matter itself. Attraction, which throws so many billion globes into an endless race, would not add an atom to it, and yet, she is the great fertilizing and inexhaustible force that no prodigality so much as dents, since she is the permanent property of bodies. It is she who initiates the whole celestial mechanics, and throws the worlds into their endless wanderings. She is rich enough to put the stars in motion, allowing them to convert it into heat by the shock that shall revive them.

Such encounters between sidereal cadavers colliding into resurrection would easily come across as a disturbance of the established order.—A disturbance! But what would become of the world if the ancient and dead suns with their string of defunct planets continued indefinitely their funeral procession, reinforced every night with the arrival of new funerals? All the sources of light and of life that shine in the heavens would extinguish gradually, like the luminaries of a light show. Eternal darkness would wash upon the universe.

The high temperatures encountered within matter at the beginning cannot have any other source than motion, the permanent force, where all the other forces originate. The sublime achievement of making a sun flourish again belongs only to the queen of all forces. Any other origin is impossible. Gravitation alone renews the worlds in the same way as it directs and maintains them thanks to motion. This, in fact, is an instinctive truth, almost as much as it is a rational and empirical one.

Indeed, experience unfolds before our very eyes every day; it is for us to watch and to draw the necessary conclusions. What is an ærolith bursting into flames and dissolving as it hisses through the air if not a small-scale image of how motion turns into heat to create a sun? Isn't this corpuscle diverted from its course to invade the atmosphere a disturbance as well? What was the normal course of action? And in the midst of this cloud of asteroids, flying with astronomical speed on their orbital path, why does one depart from the rest? What is the order and normality of this rule?

There is not one place in the universe where the disturbance of this so-called harmony is not flagrant at every moment. In fact, the absence of such disturbance would only amount to stagnation and decomposition. The laws of gravity have millions of unexpected side effects propelling a shooting star here and a sun-star there. Why exclude them from the general harmony? Such accidents displease us, and yet, we are born from them! They are the enemies of death, the prodigal sources of universal life. It is only thanks to a permanent failure of its order that gravity rebuilds and repopulates the globes. The good order we are so keen on would only abandon the planets to be swallowed into nothingness.

The universe is eternal, the stars are perishable, and since they form all matter, every one of them has passed through billions of existences. Gravity, thanks to its resurrecting shocks, divides, blends, and kneads them incessantly to the point that every one of them is a compound of the dust of all the others. Every inch of the ground that we walk has been part of the whole universe. But it is a mute witness, and it does not breathe a word of what it was given to behold in Eternity.

Spectral analysis, by revealing the presence of *simple bodies* in the stars, only reveals part of the truth. It tells the rest, little by little, through the progress of experimentation. Two important observations: the densities of our planets are variable. Yet, that of the sun is its very precise proportional sample, and thereby, it remains a faithful representation of the primitive nebula. In all likelihood, the same is the case on all stars. When the stars are atomized into a sidereal encounter, all their substances fuse into the gaseous mass that springs from the shock. Then, the organizing activity of the nebula slowly separates them, according to the laws of gravity.

In every stellar system, we should therefore see planets scaled in the same order, according to their densities, so that the planets' resemblance may result not from their sharing the same sun, but from their sharing the same rank in their specific system. Accordingly, the planets do possess identical conditions of heat, light, and density. As regards the stars, they all share an equal composition, insofar as they reproduce the mixtures that have resulted from billions of shocks and endless atomization. By contrast, the planets result from the separation between densities. Indeed, the stello-planetary mixtures, pre- pared by the Infinite herself, are far more complete and homogenous than any drug one would obtain after three generations of pharmacists had applied their pistols on it over the course of a full century.

Already I hear voices exclaim: "How does one take the liberty to suppose that the heavens harbor such a perpetual torment, which devours the stars, under the pretense of remodeling them, and which strikes such a blow to the regularity of gravitation? Where are the proofs of such shocks and of those resurrective conflagrations? Men have always admired the imposing majesty of the celestial motions, and it is now suggested we should replace such a beautiful order with permanent disorder! Who has ever spotted any sign of such a tohu-bohu anywhere?

Astronomers unanimously proclaim the invariability of the phenomena of attraction. In spite of everyone's recognition that attraction absolutely warrants stability, and security, we now witness a surge of theories that intend to build it into a maker of cataclysms. The experience garnered throughout the centuries and universal observation both energetically refute such hallucinations.

So far the changes observed in the stars are only irregularities, most of which are periodical and exclude therefore any suggestion of catastrophe. The star of the constellation of Cassiopeia in 1572,[73] like the star of Kepler in 1604,[74] has shone only of a temporary glow, which makes them irreconcilable with the hypothesis of volatilization. It appears that the universe is quite peaceful and follows its path noiselessly. For five to six thousand years, mankind has witnessed the spectacle of the Sky. It has not observed any serious trouble there. The comets have only ever caused fear but never any harm. Six thousand years, that is considerable! The reach of the telescope, too, is considerable. Neither time, nor extension, has shown anything. Such gigantic upheavals are mere dreams."

Nothing was seen, that is true, but only because nothing can be seen. Although frequent in the universe, such scenes are not performed before any audience. The observations made on the glowing stars apply only to the stars of our celestial province, contemporaneous to the sun, which remain in its company and therefore share its destiny. We are not permitted to affirm the monotonous tranquility of the universe on the basis of the calm we observe in our surroundings. The rejuvenating conflagrations have no witnesses. If ever they happen to be glimpsed, it is at the end of a telescope that shows them as a nearly imperceptible glow. The telescope thus reveals thousands of such glows. By the time our provinces become the stage of such dramas, their populations will have moved away long ago.

The incidents of Cassiopeia in 1572, of Kepler's star in 1604, are nothing but secondary phenomena. One is free to attribute them to a hydrogen eruption, or to the fall of a comet on the star, causing an explosion of ephemeral flames, like a glass of oil or alcohol spilling into a furnace. In this case, this would mean that the comets would be nothing but combustible gas. Who knows and why does it matter? Newton believed that they fueled the sun. Are we willing to generalize the hypothesis, and consider such vagrant wigs as the habitual food of all the stars? Frugal meals they are! And clearly incapable of either lighting up or reviving the torches of the world.

Again, we are left with the problem of the birth and death of the glowing stars. Whoever has set them in flames? And who replaces them once they cease to glow? Not one atom of matter can be created, and if the departed stars do not light up again, then the universe extinguishes. I challenge anyone to solve this dilemma: "Either the resurrection of the stars, or universal death…" It is the third time that I am repeating this. All that remains is that the sidereal world is alive indeed, and that since every star has in general the life span of a lightning bolt, it follows that all of the stars have already finished and started over billions of times. I have explained how. And still, the idea of the collision between globes traveling across space with the violence of lightning is found to be extraordinary. There is nothing extraordinary except for this amazement itself.

Indeed, such globes are running straight at each other and avoid collision only thanks to some artifice. Yet they cannot step aside indefinitely. Whoever seeks each other shall find each other.

All of this entitles us to conclude that the composition of the universe is unified, which does not mean that there is any "unity of substance." The 64... —let us say, the 100—*simple bodies* that make up our earth also constitute all of the globes with no exception (minus the comets, which remain an undecipherable and inconsequential myth and which, anyway, are not globes). Nature therefore has little diversity of materials at its disposal. Admittedly, she knows how to make the most of them and one remains dumbstruck at the sight of her drawing fire, water, vapor, and ice from simple bodies like hydrogen and oxygen. Chemistry knows a lot about this, although she is far from knowing all there is to know. In spite of this ability however, 100 elements leave a very tight margin after the works are completed. Let's cut to the chase.

All celestial bodies, without exception, have one single origin, the blaze resulting from collisions. Every star is a solar system born out of a nebula once volatilized by an encounter. It is the center of a group of planets already formed, or in formation. The role of the star is simple: it is a source of light and heat, which lights up, shines, and extinguishes itself. Once solidified by cooling, planets alone possess the privilege of organic life. This life draws its source in the heat and light of the hearth, and with it, it becomes extinguished. The composition and the mechanism of all stars is identical. Only the volume, the shape, and the density are variable. The entire universe is set up, functions, and lives according to this plan. There is nothing more uniform.

## VII. Analysis and Synthesis of the Universe

At this point, one becomes justified in using obscure language, as the question now at hand is itself obscure. One cannot fondle the infinite with language. One shall therefore be permitted to take over one's thought several times. Necessity excuses repetition.

The first difficulty is to find oneself face to face with Arithmetics, very rich in names of numbers, of a richness that is unfortunately quite ridiculous in its forms. The trillions, quadrillions, sextillions, etc., are farcical, and on top of this, to most readers they evoke less than a familiar and common word, which is the common way to express great numbers: *Billion*. In astronomy, how- ever, this word is nothing much and in terms of the infinite, it is nearly a zero. Unfortunately, it is precisely when it comes to the infinite that it makes its appearance under our pen. The infinite takes its lies beyond the possible; it lies even when it is simply a matter of the *indefinite*. In the following pages, figures, although they are the only language available, always narrowly miss their target, or fall into meaninglessness. It is neither their fault nor mine, it is the fault of the subject: Arithmetics does not suit it.

Thus, nature has one hundred *simple bodies* at its disposal to craft its entire works and mold them into uniform shape: "the stello-planetary system."

Nothing but stellar systems can be built, and a hundred *simple bodies* are the sole materials; this is a lot of labor and few tools. Admittedly, with such a monotonous plan and such a small variety of elements, it is difficult to engender enough different combinations to populate the infinite. Resorting to repetitions becomes necessary.

It is contended that nature never repeats itself, and that no two men, or two leaves, are identical. In a pinch this may be possible for the men of our earth, whose total number is quite restricted and divided into several races. But there are thousands of identical oak leaves, and billions of grains of sand.

There is no doubt that the one hundred *simple bodies* can make for a frightening number of *different* stello-planetary combinations. The Xs and the Ys would barely suffice to bring this calculation to its end. The long and the short of it is that this number is not even indefinite; it is finite. It has a fixed limit. Once this limit is reached, there is no going further and this limit becomes that of the universe, which, therefore, is not infinite. The celestial bodies, despite their ineffable multitude, would occupy only a point in space. Is this tolerable? Matter is eternal. One cannot imagine for one second a place where it would not have been molded into regular globes, submitted to the laws of gravitation, and on top of this, this privilege would be the property of a few unfinished sketches lost in the middle of the vacuum! A shack, lying at the heart of the infinite! This is absurd. We pose as a principle the infinity of the universe as a consequence of the infinity of space.

One cannot demand the impossible from nature. The uniformity of its method is visible everywhere and precludes the existence of infinite and exclusively original creations. Its number is bound in principle by the very finite number of the *simple bodies*. They are, as it were, *type-combinations*, whose endless *repetitions* fill up space. *Different, differentiated, distinct, primordial, original, special*, all these words express the same idea and therefore, to us, they are synonyms with the expression *type-combinations*. Establishing their number would be a task that algebra could fulfill if only the lack in data didn't make the problem indeterminate, that is to say unsolvable. Besides, this indeterminacy is not equivalent to the infinite any more than it leads into it. Every *simple body* is surely available in infinite quantity, since between all of them, they make up the whole of matter. But what is not infinite is the diversity of the elements, which does not exceed a hundred. Even if there were a thousand of them—which is not the case—the number of *type-combinations* would be formidable but, unable to reach the infinite, it would remain insignificant when it comes to it. We can therefore consider as established the incapacity of these elements to populate extension with *original types*.

It remains that we have established one point: the universe is made up of organic units which are the *stello-planetary* group, or simply *stellar*, or *planetary*, or even *solar*, since all four words are equally suited and their meanings are identical. The universe is made up entirely of an infinite series of such systems, all coming from a volatilized nebula that was condensed into a sun and planets. These last bodies, after being successively cooled down, travel around the central hearth and are kept ablaze by its formidable size. They must therefore move within the limits of attraction of their sun, and are unable to stray outside of the circumference of the primitive nebula that has engendered them. Therefore, their number is greatly restricted. It depends on the original breadth of the nebula. In our case, we find nine of them: Mercury, Venus, the Earth, Mars (the aborted planet) represented by its snatches, Jupiter, Saturn, Uranus and Neptune. Let us make it a dozen, by including three unknown ones. Their intervals increase in such a progression that it becomes difficult to extend further the limits of our group.

There is no doubt that the sizes of other stellar systems vary, but they definitely remain within proportions strongly circumscribed by the laws of equilibrium. One suggests that Sirius is one hundred and fifty times larger than the sun. How do we know? So far, it only exhibits problematic parallaxes, which are worthless. What is more, since the telescope does not magnify stars, only the eye appreciates them, so we can only estimate appearances determined by various causes. Thus, one doesn't see what entitles anyone to attribute to them diverse sizes or even any size at all. They are suns, that is all. If our sun governs over twelve celestial bodies, why would its colleagues possess much greater kingdoms?—"Why not?" one may ask. And indeed, the answer justifies the question.

Let us grant such large kingdoms. Even then the chances of diversity remain fairly weak. What do they consist of? The main one lies within the inequality of the nebulæ's volumes, which induce corresponding inequalities in the size and number of the planets within their factory. Then there are the inequalities in the shocks that modify the speed of the rotation and translation, the flattening of the poles, the slanting of the axis on the ecliptic, etc., etc.

Let us also mention the causes for similarities. One unique formation and mechanism provides the usual background: a star, the condensation of a nebula, and the center of several planetary orbits, scaled over certain intervals. Furthermore, spectral analysis reveals the unity of composition of celestial bodies. We find the same familiar elements everywhere; the universe is nothing but an ensemble of families united in flesh and in blood throughout. We find the same matter, classified and organized by the same method, in the same order. Background and government are identical. There is enough here to seriously restrict the dissimilarities and to open wide the doors of the Menæchmi.[75] Nonetheless, it is worth repeating that these data may produce an unimaginably large number of *different* combinations of planetary systems. Are such numbers infinite? No, since they are all made up of a hundred *simple bodies*, a negligible number.

The infinite is in the domain of geometry and it has nothing to do with algebra. Algebra is sometimes a game; geometry never. Algebra searches blindly like a mole. Only at the end of this groping around does it reach a result that is often a pretty formula, and sometimes a mystification. Geometry never ventures into the shadows, it keeps us staring into the three dimensions, and they do not give in to sophisms and sleights of hand. It addresses us thus: "Look at these thousands of globes, in this narrow corner of the universe, and remember their history. A conflagration pulled them out of the bosom of death and launched them into space, as immense nebulæ, the origins of a new Milky Way. Let us observe the one and we shall uncover the destiny of all."

The resurrective shock has blended together all the *simple bodies* of the nebula. Condensation separated them again before classifying them by way of the laws of gravity operating in each planet and in the ensemble of each group. The light portions are dominant in the peripheral planets, the dense ones in the central planets. Hence, the proportion of *simple bodies*, and even the total volume of globes, the necessary tendency of planets of the same rank to be similar across all stellar systems; greatness and lightness gradually spread, from the capital to the frontiers; smallness and density increase, from the frontiers to the capital. We can now catch a glimpse of the conclusion. We already know that the uniformity of the way the celestial bodies are created and the communality of their elements entail resemblances between the globes that are more than fraternal. This increasing parity in the constitution of the globes must obviously lead into the frequency of identity. The Menæchmi turn body-doubles.

Such is our basis for affirming the limitation of *differentiated* combinations of matter and, consequently, their inability to sow celestial bodies throughout the fields of space. In spite of their multitude, these combinations are limited and, therefore, they must repeat themselves in order to attain the infinite. Nature prints a billion copies of each of its works. In the texture of the stars, similarity and repetition are the rule, dissimilarity and diversity, the exception.

Once we come to grips with such numbers, how are we to formulate them except by way of figures, their only interpreters? However, these interpreters by default are unfaithful and powerless; unfaithful, when it comes to the *type-combinations* whose number is limited; powerless and vacuous, as soon as we talk about the *infinite repetitions* of these combinations. In the case of the original combinations or types, the figures are arbitrary, vague, picked at random, without any sort of value, even approximate. A thousand, a hundred thousand, a million, a trillion, etc., etc., all are erroneous, but the error is more or less severe, that is all. In the case of the *infinite repetitions*, on the contrary, any figure becomes absolute nonsense, since it attempts to express the inexpressible.

In truth, it should not be a matter for real numbers: they are, for us, only a figure of speech. Only two elements are present: the *finite* and the *infinite*. Our thesis claims that the one hundred *simple bodies* are unable to support the formation of an *infinite* number of *original* combinations. Therefore, the conflict opposes nothing other than the *finite* represented by indeterminate numbers, and the *infinite* represented by a conventional figure.

*Celestial* bodies are therefore divided between *originals* and *copies*. The *originals* are the ensembles of globes, each of which forms a special type. The *copies* are the *repetitions*, *exemplars* or *proofs* of this type. The number of *original types* is restricted, the number of *copies* or repetitions, infinite. It is by way of this latter number that the infinite constitutes itself. Each type carries behind it an army of body-doubles in limitless numbers.

As regards the first class or category, that of the *types*, the diverse numbers, available at will, cannot and will not pretend to any accuracy; all they really mean is *a lot*. As regards the second class, that is, the *copies*, *repetitions*, *exemplars*, and *proofs* (all synonyms), we will use only the term *billion*; it will be taken to mean *infinite*.

It may be conceived that the stars could exist in infinite numbers and still reproduce only one *type*. Let us assume for a second that all the stellar, material, and personal systems are an absolute copy of ours, planet by planet, without an iota of difference. This collection of *copies* would be an infinite in itself. There would be only one *type* for the entire universe. Of course, such is not the case. The number of *type-combinations* is incalculable, yet *finite*.

On the basis of the facts and demonstrations developed above, our thesis affirms that the diversity of sidereal combinations is unable to reach the infinite. O! If only the elements of matter were themselves infinitely diverse, if one could convince oneself that the composition of the remote stars has nothing in common with our earth, that nature operates everywhere with the unknown, then one could concede the infinite all one wants. However, thirty years ago already, it was thought that the infinity of the celestial bodies involved the existence of a thousand copies of our planet. Only at the time this opinion was a mere matter of instinct and rested exclusively on the awareness of the *infinite*. Spectral analysis has totally changed the situation and opened the doors for reality to rush in.

The illusion of fantastical structures has failed. There is no other material than the hundred of *simple bodies* anywhere, and two thirds of them lie before us. It is with this meager assortment that the universe must be made again and again, relentlessly. Mr. Haussmann had just that many at his disposal when he set out to rebuild Paris. Indeed, he had the very same ones. It is not diversity that shines through his buildings. Nature, which also demolishes in order to rebuild, is a more successful architect.[76] It is able to draw such wealth from its poverty that we even hesitate before attributing a limit to the originality of its productions.

Let us *restrict* the problem. Suppose that all stellar systems have the same life span, a thousand billion years for example. Let us also hypothesize that they begin and end together, at the very same minute. We know that all of these groups, which as it were share the same blood, the same flesh, the same bone structure, develop also according to the same method. In the various systems, planets are arranged symmetrically according to their degrees of resemblance and those similarities push them at the same time towards identity. One hundred *simple bodies* are the only materials of an essentially unified ensemble, and they are shared throughout. Are they capable of providing a *different* and *special* combination for each globe, that is to say, an infinite number of *distinct originals*? Certainly not, since the diversity of all the species determining the different combinations depends on a very restricted number: *one hundred*. The *differentiated* celestial bodies or *types* are therefore reduced to a limited number, and the infinity of the globes can only arise from the infinity of *repetitions*.

Thus, it appears that the original combinations run out before attaining the infinite. A myriad of different stello-planetary systems circulate in a province of space, for all they could populate is a mere province. Will matter satisfy herself with this and restrict herself to a mere point in the sky? Is she going to satisfy herself with one thousand, ten thousands, one hundred thousands such points in order to add an insignificance to her meager kingdom? No. Its calling, its law, is the infinite. It shall not let vacuum overcome it. Space shall not become its dungeon. It shall invade it and vitalize it. Why, anyway, wouldn't the infinite be a universally-shared privilege? the property of the sprout and the flour mite as well as that of the great Whole?

Such is the truth that results from such vast questions. Let us now set aside the hypothesis that triggered the demonstration. Obviously, the solar systems are not contemporaneous to each other. Far from it: their ages mix and cross over in all directions and at every moment, from the furnace that gave birth to the nebula until the death of the star, and further until the shock that will resurrect it.

Let us set aside the *original* stellar systems for a moment, let us focus on the earth. We shall connect it shortly to one of these, our solar system, where the latter belongs and which rules its destiny. It is well understood that our thesis grants no infinite personal distinction to man anymore than to animals or things. In itself, mankind is ephemeral. It is the globe its mother that includes it within her own rightful infinity in time and space. Each of our body-doubles is the child of an earth and each earth is the body-double of the actual earth. We are part of the copy. The lookalike-earth reproduces exactly everything that is found on ours and, consequently, it reproduces each individual, with its family, its house (for those who have one), and all the events of its life. It is a duplicate of our globe, both as content and as container. Nothing is missing.

The stellar systems scale their planets around the sun in an order determined by the laws of gravity and analogous creations therefore occupy a symmetrical place in each group. The earth is the third planet from the sun, and there is no doubt that this position results from its particular characteristics in size, density, sphere, etc. There are surely millions of stellar systems that come close to ours with respect to the number and the disposition of its stars. This is because the procession is strictly positioned according to the laws of gravitation. In all the groups of eight to twelve planets there is a strong chance that the third one would resemble the earth; all are variable, the distance from the sun, an essential condition as it gives light and heat in equal measure. Just like the volume and the mass, the slanting of the axis over the ecliptic. All the same, if the nebula was more or less equivalent to ours, there is every reason to think it would follow the same developments.

Let us assume degrees of diversity so great that they reduce the parallel to a simple analogy. One may come across a billion such earths before they encounter perfect resemblance. Like us, all these globes will exhibit terraced landscapes, a flora, a fauna, some seas, an atmosphere, some humans. But the length of geological periods, the distribution of water, the distribution of the continents, of the islands and of human and animal species, will offer innumerable diversity. Let us move on.

An earth is finally born when our humanity appears, displaying its races, its migrations, its struggles, its empires, its catastrophes. All these adventures will change the fate of mankind, and send it down some paths that are not those of our globe. At every second of every minute, thousands of different directions offer themselves to mankind. It chooses one and relinquishes the others forever. How many left and right swerves contribute to altering individuals, history! This is not yet our past. Let us set aside these blurry simulacra. They shall follow their own path anyway and become worlds in their own right.

We are making progress however. Here is a comprehensive copy, complete with things and people. Not a stone, not a tree, not a creek, not an animal, not a man, not an incident is absent from its rightful place and minute. We are before a genuine earth-double... until today in any case. For tomorrow, events and men shall resume their journey.

From now on, only the unknown is before us. Like our earth's past, its future will change directions millions of times. The past is a *fait accompli*; it belongs to us. The future shall come to an end only when the globe dies. Until then, every second will bring its new bifurcation, the road taken and the road that could have been taken. Whatever it may be, the road that must bring the existence of our very planet to completion has already been traveled billions of times. This road is nothing but a copy printed in advance by the centuries.

Human variants are not determined by events only. Show me a man who is not at one point in his life before two possible career paths. Although his individuality would remain unchanged the one he leaves aside would make his life very different. One career leads to misery, shame, and slavery. The other leads to glory, to freedom. Here, a charming wife and happiness all around; there, a shrew and a life of desolation. I speak for both sexes. We take such and such option by chance or by choice; no matter: no one escapes fatality. On the other hand, fate has no grip on the infinite, for the infinite knows no alternatives and has room for everything. On one earth, Man is found following the road relinquished by his body-double on the other. His existence doubles out, with one globe for each, and then it bifurcates a second time, a third time, and a thousand times. Thus, one man possesses complete body-doubles as well as an innumerable number of variations who multiply and always represent his person, but who borrow only scraps of his destiny. We are, somewhere else, everything that we could have been down here. In addition to our whole life, to our birth and death, which we experience on a number of earths, we also live ten thousand different versions of it on other earths.

The great events of our globe have their counterpart, especially when fatality plays a role. The English may have often lost the Battle of Waterloo on the globes where their opponents did not make Grouchy's mistake.[77] This battle was narrowly won. On the other hand, not everywhere does Bonaparte always win at Marengo, which he won on this earth by a mere fluke.[78]

I can already hear the clamors: "What folly this is, coming straight from Bedlam! What? Billions of copies of analogous earths! Other billions for the nearly similar! Hundred of millions for the foolish actions and the crimes of mankind! And then, thousands of millions more for all the individual fantasies. Every good or bad mood of ours seen as owning a special sample of globe, at its orders, and every celestial crossroad as being jammed with our body-doubles!"

No, no! These doubles are not clustered anywhere. They are even very rare, although they exist by billions, that is to say, beyond count. Our telescopes, which have a handsome field to scan, would be unable to find one single copy of our planet, assuming it was visible at all. It would take a thousand, perhaps a hundred thousand times this field, until we make such an encounter. In a universe made up of a thousand million stellar systems, who knows if one could find even one copy of our group or of one of its members? Yet, their number is infinite. In the beginning, we said, "Let every word denote the most frightening of distances, it would still take us billions and billions of centuries of talking at a rate of one word per second in order to express a distance which, as far as the infinite is concerned, is only an insignificance."

Such a thought is in application here. As *special types*, each of which exists in a single copy, the thousands of *differing* variations of the earth would occupy only a point in space. Each one must be repeated to the *infinite* before it accounts for anything. The exact body-double of our earth—the one replicating it from the day of its birth to its death, then again in its resurrection—exists a billion times, for every second of its duration. This is its destiny as a *repetition* of an *original* combination, and it is shared by all the *repetitions* of the other *types*.

Affirming that there is a duplicated offprint of our terrestrial existence, complete with every single one of its inhabitants, from the grain of sand to the emperor of Germany, may seem to reveal a boldness that borders on the fantastic, especially when it comes to a copy assumed to be printed by billions. The author, of course, finds his own arguments excellent, since he repeated them already five to six times, without concern about the future. To him, it is hardly conceivable that nature, performing the same labor with the same materials and according to the same pattern, avoid casting its iron in the same mold. It is the contrary, in fact, that would be surprising.

As regards the large print run, there is no need for caution when it comes to the infinite: it is rich. However demanding one is, the infinite possesses more than every demand, more than every dream. Besides, this shower of *copies* does not fall on any single location. It is scattered across immeasurable spaces. It is of little importance to us whether our body-doubles are our neighbors. Assuming they lived on the moon, this would not make our conversation with them any easier, or our knowledge of them more complete. It is even flattering to know oneself to be over there, far away, miles from anywhere, in one's slippers, reading a newspaper, or witnessing the Battle of Valmy taking place, at this very minute, in thousands of French Republics.[79]

Imagine some compassionate land, at the other end of the infinite, where the royal prince, arriving too late upon Sadowa, let Benedek win his battle!…[80] But here comes Pompey, having just lost at Pharsalus. Poor man! He now seeks comfort in Alexandria, next to his good friend king Ptolemy… Cæsar will laugh!…[81] Well, just about! He is in the middle of the senate, receiving his twenty-two stabs… Bah! it is his daily lot since the non-beginning of the world and he receives them with unfazed spirit. Admittedly, his body-doubles do not warn him. That is the terrible part! No one can warn anyone else. If only it were permitted to provide access to the history of our life, complete with a few good tips, to the doubles we have in space, we would spare them a lot of foolishness and sorrow…

All of this, joking aside, is very serious. It is not a matter of anti-lions, of anti-tigers, or of eyes at the tip of one's tail; it is a matter of mathematics and positive facts. I defy nature not to manufacture billions of solar systems everyday since the origins of time, in exact compliance with the characteristics of our own material and personal solar system. I shall allow it to exhaust all calculations of probabilities without exception. Once it reaches the end of its tether, I'll fold it back unto the infinite and urge it to fulfill its function; that is to say, to produce copies endlessly. I must refrain from justifying this by appealing to the beauty of the samples and arguing that it would be a great pity not to multiply them to saturation. On the contrary, I find it unhealthy and barbaric to poison space with such a jumble of fetid countries.

Useless observations anyway. Nature neither knows nor practices morality. What she does, she doesn't do on purpose. She works blindfolded, destroys, creates, transforms. Nothing else concerns her. With eyes shut, she applies probability calculus better than mathematicians explain it with their eyes wide open. Not one variation eludes her, not one possibility lies unused at the bottom of the urn. She draws every number. When there is nothing left in the sack, she opens the repetition box, a bottomless barrel this one, which never runs out, as opposed to the barrel of the Danaids, which could never be filled.[82]

Such has been the way of matter, ever since matter was matter, which was not yesterday. She has been following a unified plan determined by the one hundred *simple bodies* that never decrease or increase by one atom; all that is left for her to do is to repeat a certain number of *different* combinations endlessly. These are therefore called *primordial*, *original*, et cetera; matter's workshop produces only stellar systems.

The mere fact that any celestial body exists now proves that it has always existed and will always exist, not in its current individuality—which is temporary and ephemeral—, but in an infinite series of similar individualities that recur throughout the centuries. Every celestial body therefore belongs to one of the original combinations made possible by the various arrangements of the one hundred *simple bodies*. It is identical to its previous incarnations, to the point that when placed in the same conditions, it lives and shall live exactly the same life that its previous avatars did both overall and in detail.

Every celestial body is a repetition of an *original* combination, or *type*. No new *type* can be created. The number of *types* has necessarily been exhausted since the very beginning of things,—although things did not have an origin. This means that a fixed number of *original* combinations exists in all eternity and is not able to increase or reduce any more than matter itself. It is unchangeable and shall remain so until the end of things, and things cannot end any more than they could begin. There is eternity for the actual *types*, in the past as in the future, and every celestial body without exception is a *type* repeated to the infinite in time and in space. Such is the nature of reality.

Our earth, as well as other celestial bodies, is the *repetition* of a primordial *combination*, which replicates itself identically every time, and which exists simultaneously in billions of identical copies. Every copy is born, lives, and dies in turn. Every second that passes sees them being born and dying by the billions. All the material things, as well as all the organized beings, follow the very same sequence, in the same place, at the very same minute on the surface of this planet as they do on the surface of its body-doubles, that is to say, the other earths. Therefore, all the facts having taken place on our globe, or having yet to take place before the time of its death, are accomplished at the exact identical on its billions of copies. And since this is the case for every stellar system, the entire universe is a permanent reproduction, without end, of an ever renewed and ever identical material and personnel.

Does the identity of two planets involve the identity of their solar systems? Certainly, that of the two suns is absolutely necessary, as anything else would involve changing their conditions of existence, taking the two stars down different paths in spite of their original identity, which is unlikely anyway. But at the scale of each solar group, is the similarity of any single globe dependent on the similarity of all of the other globes with their homologues, as determined by their position in the system? Must we have double Mercury, double Mars, double Neptune, et cetera, et cetera? The lack of data makes this question impossible to answer.

Surely, these bodies are influenced by each other, and say, the absence of Jupiter, or its ninety percent shrinking, would impose noticeable modification upon its neighbors. However, distance softens such causes and it can even cancel them out. What is more, the sun rules alone, as light and as heat, and when we recall that its mass is to its planetary procession like 744 is to 1, it seems that this enormous power of attraction reduces any competing one to nothing. However, this is not the case. The planets do have a verifiable influence on the earth.

In any case, this is an inconsequential question that has no bearing on our thesis. If it were only possible that two earths be identical, in spite of the planets around them being different, then it is a done deal, because nature misses no possible combination. If it is not possible, then so what. Let earth-doubles require solar system-doubles as their *sine qua non*, then. All this implies is the existence of millions of stellar groups where our globe, in place of exact body-doubles, possesses a diversity of Menæchmi with various degrees of likeness, *original* combinations, repeated to the infinite, just like all the others.

All the same, the existence of infinite numbers of perfectly identical solar systems easily satisfies the demands of the obligatory program. They constitute an *original type*. There, we find every planet perfectly identical to its correspondent. Mercury is the body-double of Mercury, Venus of Venus, the Earth of the Earth, etc. Billions of those systems are scattered across space, as *repetitions* of the same type.

Have any of the *differentiated* combinations originated as identical ones whose differences appeared after birth? We must make a distinction: it is quite unacceptable to say that such matter spontaneously mutates thusly. The first minute of a celestial body determines the whole series of its future material transformations. Nature has only inflexible and immutable laws. As long as these laws are alone at the helm, the celestial bodies shall follow a fateful and fixed path. But variations are introduced with the animated beings and their will, that is to say, their caprices. As soon as humans are involved, fantasy in particular is also involved. Not that humans can do much in the way of changing the planet. Their greatest efforts do not even move a molehill, even though this does not prevent them from posturing as conquerors infatuated with their own genius and power. Matter wipes out the works of these Myrmidons soon enough, just as soon as they cease to defend them against it.[83] Go and seek the famous cities of Nineveh, Babylon, Thebes, Memphis, Persepolis, Palmyra, all squirming with millions of feverishly agitated inhabitants. What is left of them? Not even ruins. Grass and sand now cover their tombs. No sooner have we neglected the works of the humans for a minute than nature begins to peacefully demolish them, and should we happen to delay, we find her flourishing on its wrecks again.

Men do not disturb matter, not very much, but they disturb themselves a great deal. The turbulences of man never affect the natural workings of physical phenomena in any serious manner, but they do turn their own kind upside down. We must therefore factor in this subversive influence that changes the course of individual destinies, destroys and modifies the animal species, tears nations apart, and collapses empires. Of course, all this violence takes place without leaving as much as a scratch on the skin of the earth. The so-called sovereign presence of human intruders would not leave a trace once men have disappeared, and this would be enough to return nature to its barely touched virginity.

It is only amongst themselves that humans make victims and bring about huge changes. The winds of passion and the struggles of interests agitate them with more violence than the tempests that move the ocean. How greatly different are the fates of the races, even though they have begun their careers with the same personnel, as required by the identical material conditions of their planets! If we include the mobility of individuals, the hundreds of turbulences that continually carry them off their path, we shall easily reach sextillions of sextillions of variants in mankind. But only the one *original* combination of matter that constitutes our planetary system is able to provide billions of earths by *repetition*, therefore ensuring that the sextillions of different Mankinds, engendered through the effervescences of men, be given body-doubles. The first year of the voyage shall only produce ten variations perhaps, the second one ten thousand, the third will produce millions, and so on, with a *crescendo* proportional to the progress which, as we know, expresses itself in extraordinary ways.

Those different human groups have only one thing in common: duration. This is because even though they are born out of *copies* of the same *original type*, they can each compose their own version in their own way. The number of such particular histories, however large, is always a *finite* number, and we know that the *primordial* combination is infinite, by *repetition*. Each particular history, as it represents one single community, is printed out in a billion identical *copies*, and as a member of this community, each individual therefore possesses billions of body-doubles. We know that every man has the ability to be present on several variations at a time, due to the changes in the paths followed by his body-doubles on their respective earths. Hence, these changes double life out, but personality is left untouched.

Let us sum up: matter, compelled to build only nebulæ, transforms into stello-planetary groups, yet, in spite of its fecundity, it cannot exceed a certain number of *special* combinations. Each *type* is a stellar system that endlessly repeats itself, for this is the only way for it to populate space. Our sun, with its procession of planets, is one of the original combinations, and like all the others, it is printed out in a billion copies. Each of these copies is a natural part of an earth identical to ours, a body-double as far as its material constitution is concerned, and therefore engenders the same vegetable and animal species as are found on the earth's surface.

All Mankinds, identical at the time of hatching, follow, each on their own planet, the road laid out by the passions, and each individual's particular influence contributes to designing that road. As a result, in spite of the constant identity of the beginning, Mankind does not have the same personnel on all similar globes, and each of the globes have, as it were, its own particular Mankind, each of them comes from the same source, and began at the same point, but branches out into a thousand paths, finally leading into different lives and different histories.

But the restricted number of inhabitants on each earth does not allow the variations of Mankind to exceed a determinate number. Hence, however unheard-of it may be, the number of *particular* human communities is *finite*. Therefore, it is nothing in comparison to the *infinite* quantity of identical earths, all of which belong to the *typical* solar combination. And every single one of them possessed a similar Human race at the beginning, even though they later became continually modified. As a result, every earth—containing one of these *particular* human communities that are the result of continual modifications—must repeat itself billions of times in order to satisfy the requirements of the infinite. Hence the billions of earths, absolutely identical, personally and materially, where neither a blade of hay, nor a thousandth of a second, nor a spider's thread, vary in either time or space. Such terrestrial variations and human communities behave like *original* stellar systems. Their number is limited, because it is made of elements whose numbers themselves are *finite* (such as the number of men on one earth), just like the *original* stellar systems have a *finite* number of elements, the one hundred *simple bodies*. But every variation issues billions of copies of itself.

Such is the common destiny of our planets, Mercury, Venus, the Earth, etc., etc., and of the planets of all the *primordial* or *typical* stellar systems. It should be added that among these systems there are millions that resemble ours without being genuine *duplicates*, and that contain innumerable earths similarly different from those where we live but which resemble and correspond to them in the highest degree.

All those systems with all their variations and all their *repetitions* make up innumerable series of partial infinites that dissolve into the great infinite like rivers dissolve into the ocean. Let us not be alarmed at those globes pouring out of the quill by the billions. Let us not ask: where shall we find enough room for so many worlds? Instead, let's ask: where shall we find enough worlds for all this room? One may billionize till the cows come home with the infinite, it shall always ask for more.

The doctrines that are always prompt to laugh and cry will certainly mock our partial infinites and congratulate us for earning so much change with a forged coin. Indeed, when extension is denied a unique infinite, it seems harmless to grant it billions. Nothing is simpler however. Space is boundless, therefore, it may be attributed several figures, precisely because it has none. Then a sphere, now a cylinder, such is space.

Let nine saw cuttings divide a cylindrical block of wood into ten boards, perpendicularly to its axis. Let us extend in thought the circular perimeter of each of these boards to the infinite. Let us separate them, in thought again, with intervals of quadrillions of quadrillions of leagues. Here are ten perfect yet quite meager partial infinites. Every star, in our calculations, would fit comfortably, along with their distinctive domains, within each of these compartments. What is more, nothing prevents us from attaching other stars to them, and from adding up the infinite at will in this way.

Of course, such stars do not remain locked up into categories and identities. The resurrecting conflagrations blend and melt them ceaselessly. A solar system does not get born again like a phoenix out of its own combustion; on the contrary, this combustion contributes to forming different combinations. Such a volatilized system gets its revenge later, as it is given birth again through other volatilizations. Everywhere the materials are the same one hundred *simple bodies*, and since the given is the infinite, the probabilities become equalized. The result is the invariable permanence of the whole throughout the constant transformation of its parts.

If, out of concern about our *Indefinite*, Chicanery vainly attempts to force us to understand the *Infinite* and to explain it, let us refer it to the Jupiterians, who are surely endowed with a larger brain than us. No, it is a well-known fact that there is no exceeding the indefinite. This expression is nothing but our attempt to conceive of the *Infinite*. One adds space to space, and the mind comes easily to the conclusion that it is limitless. Undoubtedly, one could accumulate space for thousands of centuries, and the total would still be a *finite* number. What does that prove? It proves the *Infinite* first of all, by showing that the end cannot be attained, and then, it proves the weakness of our brain too.

Indeed, after throwing figures around to the risk of shrugging shoulders and causing laughter, we are still breathless, stuck at the first steps of the road to the infinite. The infinite is however as clear as it is impenetrable, and a word suffices to demonstrate it:

Space, filled with celestial bodies, always, endless. It is really quite simple, although incomprehensible.

Our analysis of the universe has mostly involved the staging of the planets, the sole theater of organic life. The stars remained in the background. This is because when it comes to the stars, there are no changing forms, no metamorphoses. Nothing but the chaos of the formidable fire, source of heat and light, followed by its gradual decrease and concluded in icy darkness. Nonetheless, the star is the vital hearth of the groups constituted by the condensation of the nebulæ. None other than the star classifies and regulates the system that surrounds her. In any *type-combination*, the star is unique in size and in motion. It remains constant in all the replicas of this *type*, including the planetary variations created by mankind.

Let us not imagine, indeed, that the replications of the globes happen for the sake of the body-doubles that inhabit it. The prejudice taught by education and egoism according to which we relate everything to ourselves is foolish. Nature has no concern for us. She creates stellar groups according to the available materials. Some are *originals*, others, the duplicates, have billions of copies of themselves published. Actually, there are—strictly speaking—no *originals*, that is to say earlier ones, but only diverse *types*, according to which the stellar systems are classified.

Whether the planets of those groups produce men or not, this is not nature's concern, for she has no concern at all; she does her work without worrying about the consequences. She assigns 998 *thousandths* of matter to stars where not a blade of grass, not a flour mite lives, and the rest, "*two thousandths*!" she attributes to the planets of which half, if not more, do without hosting or feeding bipeds such as us. Overall, however, she does things well, and we should not complain. Were it more modest, the lamp that lights and warms us up would promptly abandon us to eternal night, or more accurately, we would never have stepped into the light.

Only the stars would be entitled to complain, but they don't. Poor stars! Their splendid role is only sacrificial. Although they are the creators and the servants of the productive power of the planets, they do not possess it for themselves, and they must satisfy themselves with their ungrateful and monotonous career as torches. They have the glow without the benefits; it is behind them that hide the living invisible realities. These queen-slaves are, however, made of the same stuff as their lucky subjects. The hundred *simple bodies* account for all of them. But those *simple bodies* will regain their fecundity only by stripping off greatness. They are blinding flames now and one day they will be darkness and ice, and then they will return to life only as planets, after the shock that will have volatilized the procession and its queen into a nebula.

While they wait for the bliss of this downfall, the queens unknowingly govern their kingdoms by bestowing benefits onto them. They do the sowing, but not the harvesting. They have the charges, but not the benefits. Although they are masters of force, they use it only for the sake of weakness... Dear stars! You shall find few imitators.

Let us finally conclude the immanence of the smallest scraps of matter. Although their lifespan is of one second, their rebirth is boundless. The infinity in time and space is not the exclusive privilege of the universe as a whole. It also belongs to every form of matter, down to the infusoria and grains of sand.

Thus, thanks to his planet, every man possesses an endless number of doubles across space, and they live his life exactly like he lives it himself. Every man is infinite and eternal through the being of other himselves, who are not only of his actual age, but also of all *his ages*. At every second, simultaneously, he has billions of body-doubles who are being born, others who are dying, others whose ages range, from second to second, from his birth to the age of his death.

If one were to question the celestial regions in order to ask them what their secret is, billions of body-doubles would raise their eyes at the same time, with the very same question in their minds, and all these glances would fly past each other, invisible. And such questions do not fly across space only once, they do so continually. Every second of eternity has seen and shall see today's situation, that is to say billions of copies of our earth carrying our personal body-doubles.

Therefore, every one of us has lived, lives, and shall live endlessly, under the form of billions of *alter egos*. Whatever we are at every second of our life is how we will be stereotyped to a billion copies in eternity. We share the destiny of the planets, our nourishing mothers within whose bosom this inexhaustible existence accomplishes itself. The stellar systems carry us along within their immortality. Being the only organization of matter, they possess its fixity and its mobility all at once. Each of them is but a strike of lightning, but such strikes illuminate space eternally.

The universe is eternal as a whole as well as in each of its fractions, be it a star or a speck of dust. Such it is at this very minute, such it was in the past, and such it will always be, without one atom or one second of variation. There is nothing new under the sun.[84] Everything that is being accomplished has been and will be accomplished. However, although it is self-identical, the universe is not immutable or immobile; the universe of then is not the universe of now, and the universe of now will not be the one that the future will bring. On the contrary, it transforms continually. Every one of its parts is in an uninterrupted movement. Although they are destroyed here, they reproduce themselves simultaneously elsewhere, as new individuals.

The stellar systems finish and then begin again with similar elements that they obtain thanks to new alliances and to the indefatigable mechanisms of reproduction of identical copies drawn from various ruins. It is an alternation, a continuous exchange of rebirths by transformation.

The universe is at once life and death, destruction and creation, change and stability, rest and unrest. It ties itself up and unties itself endlessly, ever the same, with forever renewing beings. In spite of its constant becoming, it is engraved in bronze and relentlessly prints the same one page. As a whole as well as in detail, the universe is forever transformation and immanence.

Mankind is one of these details. It shares the mobility and the permanence of the great Whole. There is not one human being who has not been present on billions of globes, before being drowned again in the recasting crucible. In vain would one trek up the rapids of the centuries in search of a universe devoid of humans. Indeed, the universe has no beginning, and therefore, neither has mankind. It would be impossible to flow back to a time before all the celestial bodies along with ourselves, their inhabitants, had not been destroyed and replaced. In the future, likewise, there shall never pass a moment without billions of other ourselves being born, living, and dying. The human, just like the universe, is the enigma of the infinite and of eternity, and the grain of sand is equal to the human.

## VIII. Summary

The universe as a whole is composed of stellar systems. In order to create them, nature has only one hundred *simple bodies* at its disposal. In spite of the prodigious wealth that she is able to draw from these resources and of the incalculable number of combinations that make its fecundity possible, the result is surely a number as *finite* as the elements themselves, and in order to fill the expanses, nature must repeat every one of her *original* combinations or *types*.

Any celestial body, whatever it is, exists in infinite numbers in time and space, not only under one of its aspects, but such that it appears at every second of its life span, from its birth till its death. Every being great or small, live or inert, that is spread over its surface, shares the privilege of this immortality.

The earth is one of these celestial bodies. Therefore every human being is eternal at every second of its existence. That which I am writing at this moment, in a dungeon of the Fort du Taureau, I have written and shall write again forever, on a table, with a quill, under clothes and in entirely similar circumstances. And so it is for all of us.

All of these earths stumble, one after the other, into the rejuvenating flames, so as to be born again and to stumble again, in the monotonous flow of an hourglass eternally turning itself over and emptying itself. What we have is ever-old newness and ever-new oldness.

Those who are curious about extra-terrestrial life may smirk at a mathematical conclusion that grants, not only their immortality, but eternity? The number of our body-doubles is infinite in time and in space. In all honesty, one could not demand more. These body-doubles are in flesh and bones, even in trousers and vest, in crinoline and chignon. They are not ghosts, they are a piece of eternity actualized.

Yet, there is one shortcoming: there is no progress. Alas! no, these are vulgar reissues, repetitions. So too are the copies of past worlds, so too are those of future worlds. Only the chapter of bifurcations remains open to hope. Let us not forget that *everything we could have been on this earth, we are it somewhere else.*

Progress on this earth is reserved only to our nephews. They are luckier than us. All the beautiful things that our world will see, our future descendants have already seen them, are seeing them now and will see them always, of course, in the form of doubles that preceded them and will follow them. As sons of a better humanity, they have already properly humiliated and defamed us on the dead earths, in passing there after us. They continue to denigrate us on the living earths from which we have disappeared, and they will forever continue to hunt us with their scorn on the earths yet to be born.

Like them and like all the other guests of our planet, we are reborn as prisoners of the time and place which fate assigns us in the series of our planet's avatars. Our immortality is an annex of our planet's own. We are but the epiphenomena of its resurrections. Men of the nineteenth century, the hour of our appearance is fixed once and for all, and always assigns us the same incarnation. At best, it gives us the perspective of lucky variations. Nothing here to flatter the thirst for improvement much. What can we do? I haven't sought my pleasure; I have sought the truth. There is neither revelation here, nor prophet, but a simple deduction drawn from spectral analysis and the cosmogony of Laplace. These two discoveries make us eternal. Is it a blessing? Let us take advantage of it. Is it a mystification? Let us resign ourselves.

But is it not a consolation to know that at every moment, on billions of earths, we are in the company of beloved people, people who are now only a memory for us? Is it not another consolation, however, to think, that we have tasted this happiness and that we shall taste it eternally, under the guise of a body-double, of billions of body-doubles? It is truly ourselves. For many a narrow mind, those blessings by proxy provide little intoxication. They would readily exchange all the duplicates of the infinite for three or four extra years in the current edition. We are prone to clinging, in our century of disillusions and skepticism.

At heart, man's eternity by the stars is melancholic, and even sadder this estrangement of brother-worlds caused by the inexorable barrier of space. So many identical populations come to pass without having suspected each other's existence! Well, not really: this shared existence is discovered at last in the 19th century. But who shall believe it?

Moreover, so far the past represented barbarity, and the future meant progress, science, happiness, illusion! This past has witnessed the disappearance of the most brilliant civilizations on every one of our globe-doubles, they disappeared without a trace, and they will do so again, without leaving more of a trace. On billions of earths, the future will witness the very same ignorance, the very same foolishness, and the very same cruelties of our old ages!

At the present hour, the entire life of our planet, from its birth to its death, unfolds, day by day, on myriads of twin-globes, with all its crimes and misery. What we call progress is locked up on each earth and disappears with it. Always and everywhere, on the terrestrial camp, the same drama, the same set, on the same narrow stage,[85] a noisy humanity, infatuated by its own greatness, thinking itself to be the universe and inhabiting its prison like an immensity, only to drown soon along with the globe that has borne the burden of its pride with the deepest scorn. The same monotony, the same immobility in the foreign stars. The universe repeats itself endlessly and struts on its legs. Unfazed, eternity plays the same performance in the infinite.

# A Visit to Blanqui

"A Visit to Blanqui" appears in the *London Times* of April 28, 1879. It was then reprinted in several outlets worldwide, including *The New York Times* (May 10, 1879) and *The New Orleans Daily Democrat* (May 15, 1879), under a variety of titles. The interview occurred on April 25, 1879, at the Prison of Clairvaux where Blanqui was serving a sentence for his involvement with the Paris Commune of 1871 (although he was unable to participate in it physically). In the interview, Blanqui discusses his election as a member of parliament for Bordeaux, which took place on April 20th. Although his election would be invalidated on June 1st due to his legal record, Blanqui would be released on the 10th of that month.

The interview, which takes place seven years after the writing of *Eternity*, offers the reader an insight for Blanqui in vivo. Many of the impressions one may have gotten from reading *Eternity* are here confirmed. Blanqui's constant economy of words and concepts, and his sense for the definitive formulation remain as robust as before. Yet, Blanqui no longer seems concerned to dispel the impression that he is and remains an activist. Does this make *Eternity* a mere parenthesis, or should we read it as an activist text of sorts? How should the notion that "in prison, a manuscript is never your own" influence our reading of *Eternity*? Similarly, should we take Blanqui's denunciation of the Church's efforts at repressing materialism in physics cast light on the transgressive intent of the *Eternity*? Finally, should we interpret his constant talk of substitutions and replacements, built into a political program, as a remnant of his astronomical speculations?

# A Visit to Blanqui from our Paris Correspondent[86]

## Clairvaux, April 25

The hero of the day, on whom I have just been waiting, is the newly-elected representative of Bordeaux, the prisoner of Clairvaux, whom 6,000 electors wished to release by placing the will of a trifling fraction of the electoral body above the law of the land. For a fortnight so much has been heard of Blanqui and so much fanaticism and ill-faith exhibited on his account that it seemed to me the most logical thing to do was simply to go to Clairvaux, there examine this relic of militant Socialism, and see for myself what was true and what not.

I accordingly took measures for obtaining access to Blanqui. It is not necessary to detail the efforts by which I was enabled to gratify my wish. I need only say that I left Paris on Wednesday night, alighting at Bar-sur-Aube, and traveling by road affords opportunities of talking with country people, who when you are in search of anything often give the first clue to the truth. The driver told me that my journey was to no purpose, seeing that at Bar-sur-Aude, which is 15 kilometers from Clairvaux, it was known that Blanqui had left Clairvaux on Monday. As soon as the votes had been counted and it was known that

Blanqui was elected, orders had been given to set him at liberty. He had been released on Monday evening, when it was announced that the train would come in an hour late so as to prevent a crowd from collecting at the station. Thus the attempt of the Bordeaux electors to place their will above the law seemed to the inhabitants of the Aube naturally to imply the immediate release of this man, who has passed his whole life in struggling against society, in being by turns a menace and a victim. The truth is, however, that Blanqui is at Clairvaux; that the Government has no idea of setting him free; that I have just had a long conversation with him.

On arriving at Clairvaux I called on M. Dumerre, who has had charge of the prison for 11 years, and to whom I had to present the papers which were to gain me access to the prisoner. Clairvaux is composed of the penitentiary buildings, an old monastery of the Cistercian Order, of an inn on the high road, and some score of houses, whose tenants gain their livelihood by agriculture and the small retail business to which the presence of the 1,500 to 2,000 prisoners, warders, workmen, and soldiers who people the establishment gives rise. The penitentiary itself is a little industrial centre where silk, velvet, iron bedsteads, wire gauze, and mother-of-pearl buttons are manufactured for foreign customers. The labourers and artisans condemned to prison in the departments of the Marne, Haute-Marne, Aube, andc., are sent there according as their profession corresponds with the industries there carried on. M Dumerre received me with affability and gave me some preliminary information of which I stood in need.

He is a well-educated man, who has had a long experience of his difficult mission, and whose manner of expressing himself is clear and interesting. Since France passed through her trials he has had the wildest fraction of the Socialists under his eyes, for Malarties, Persuton, Luillier, Fontaine, and many others whose names are connected with the civil disasters of France have passed through Clairvaux. He sent for the chief warder and accompanied me across the first three courtyards of the establishment to the sinister-like building which forms the portion tenanted by Blanqui.

A Paris newspaper which I have just been reading asks whether Blanqui knows of his election and affirms that he has not written to his family since the 1st. Not only does Blanqui know of his election, but he has read most of the papers which discuss it, and is very angry with the *Temps*, which attributes his election in great part to the co-operation of the Bonapartists. Congratulatory letters and postcards are reaching him by dozens from all the revolutionary quarters of France, and he has already received invitations from Paris and the provinces to attend public and private meetings and make speeches. These meeting-makers are perfectly scrambling for the promise of obtaining the speeches of this Prophet of the Mountain on his delivery from long captivity. I mentioned this because not only did M. Dumarre inform me that Blanqui was perfectly up on what was passing in regard to himself, but also because it was agreed that I only came to see him on account of the noise his election was making, and because, he was to be informed, that I was the Correspondent of

*The Times*, and that it was in this capacity that I came to confer with him.

The chief warder unlocked a door and we entered the prisoner's room. This is one of the immense halls of the infirmary. Blanqui has inhabited it for several years. It is about 15 metres long, seven metres wide, and four metres in height. Five gigantic windows look out beyond the two walls on green hills crowned by a pine wood, beyond which one catches a glimpse of the Aube valley. The three side windows look out on a garden, divested at this season of the flowers which adorn it in summer. Two-thirds of the length of the hall are empty, and the prisoner's abode really commences at the fourth window. An iron bedstead, with suitable bedding, a few cane chairs, a big armchair, on which is heaped a large collection of the *Journal Officiel*, several dictionaries, historical works on the table, a mahogany card-table, and a porcelain stove surrounded by a great number of round logs of wood formed the prisoner's furniture. A good fire burnt in the grate, while, pursuant to hygienic conditions, of course, one of the tower windows was half open and let in the fresh air of one of the rare fine mornings of the season. Along the wall opposite the windows was a large, long plank covered with stencils, boxes, cans and jugs, provisions and parcels containing linen and clothes. I was able to take a look at all this at my ease, for just as we entered the room its tenant was not to be seen. A few minutes after a concealed door opened and Blanqui entered.

Never have I witnessed a greater contrast than that between the man I saw before me and the stir which his name has for the last few weeks created. There entered a short, thin, grey man in the strangest garb. He wore light sabots over dark socks; coffee-colored trousers; a coarse, unstarched linen shirt without a collar, a knitted waistcoat, buttoned at the neck, but with no other button; a silk skull-cap the worse for wear, from beneath which was a yellowish cotton handkerchief nearly covering his forehead, and some of the fringe of which was scarcely distinguishable from his thick white hair. Clutched in his trembling right hand was a small hatchet, which he had just used for chopping wood, and which he let go only toward the end of our interview. His physiognomy curiously supplemented this fanciful garb. His head is short at the lower part, broad toward the temples, and set off with a bristly white beard. His complexion is clear and rosy, his forehead broad, but low, and slightly compressed at the temples; his ears are rather delicate, his eyes long and fixed; his nose is thin at the top, broad and square below; his mouth wide, his lips red and his expression, though sometimes lit up with an agreeable smile, usually shows a kind of cynical curiosity. When, however, M. Dusserre told him who I was, and that I had come to talk with him, he lifted his singular dress with his left hand, still grasping the hatchet with his right, began to smile, and after a moment's surprise, said to me:

"— Then, every door is open to you, and you have come here to satisfy the insatiable curiosity of the great English journal?

— No, I replied; it is not mere curiosity which brings me hither. Your name is everywhere, and I come to ascertain from yourself the truth respecting you."

The Governor and Chief Warden withdrew and left us alone.

Blanqui motioned me to sit down and we took two chairs near the stove.

What feeling, I asked, did you experience on learning that you had been elected?

"— I thought it would do me good; that it was a Republican demonstration in my favour, but that I should not be released, because if I were to be released I should have been the first to profit by the arbitrary Amnesty Bill which was passed.

Why the first? Were you not condemned for insurrection of the 31st of October, 1870?

Just so.

Well, what was the insurrection of the 31st of October?

An insignificant skirmish. It ended all at once. There was not a drop of blood spilt, nor even a blow with the fist given except those I received from the National Guards and did not return. In French insurrections there has always been bloodshed. In that of the 31st of October there was none. In the courts of the Hôtel de Ville there were battalions. On both sides we made a compromise and left arm in arm. We were 12 or 15 who made the 31st of October, yet Flourens and I alone have been tried and condemned for it, nobody else being troubled about it. I have been here seven years for that. I ought to have been amnestied the first.

But, do you forget that Paris was besieged, that the Germans were at the gates, that you provoked an insurrection under the fire of the enemy, and thus, perhaps, prevented peace from being then concluded—for your insurrection broke out at the moment M. Thiers was negotiating with Prince Bismarck?

But the Germans were terribly afraid of seeing our enterprise succeed. We made the insurrection because the others would not employ the forces which Paris contained, and if we had overturned them victory would have changed sides.

I looked at him with astonishment.

Was there among you a single man of military capacity to do more than was done? Did you count on Flourens to defeat the Germans?

He would, at any rate, have done more than Trochs. He would, at least, have known how to die. Trochs was a real quack. He owed his military reputation only to his writings, and on a battlefield he would have let himself be surrounded and beaten. The 31st of October had no result; the Government began again 24 hours afterwards.

Yes, but you had destroyed confidence for ever.

One cannot destroy what has not existed. The inhabitants never had confidence in those men.

What did you do after the 31st of October?

I remained concealed at Paris until February, tried and condemned by default. In February the Commune broke out, and I was tried in March, 1872, by Bonapartists and Legitimists. All this is why I ought to have been amnestied the first. Moreover, I have had enough of prison. I have had 40 years. I began to conspire in 1831 with Barthélemy Saint-Hilaire, who has since gone over to the Right, with Bixie, who was afterwards Napoléon's Minister, and with an advocate named Plod. I alone have not changed.

Why did you conspire against Louis-Philippe?

He did not suit us. He had travestied the Revolution of July. It was the continuation of Charles X.

Why did you in 1848 make the 15th of May?

I did not make it, but it was my duty to be in it. I knew it would not turn out well. I was sent to Vincennes, but that did not prevent the rising of June.

But if you went out to-day you would do the same thing, and the same thing would happen to you?

Why do you want my convictions to alter? I have not to abdicate; moreover, there is no longer a dynasty interested in imprisoning me.

It is said you are a disciple of Babeuf, and that you would put his theories into practice.

That is mere talk. I have no theory. I am not a professor of politics of Socialism; I am a man of action. What exists is bad; something else must take its place, and gradually things will become what they ought to be. The revolutionary party will apply the necessary reforms. First and foremost, France must be unchristianized. She must be rid, not only of Catholicism, but of Christianity. The Catholics are now the masters. We have still the Inquisition. It no longer burns, but it imprisons. The magistrates sentence according to its orders. Journalists are condemned because they turn religion into derision. It ought to be allowable to turn religion into derision in the name of reason. I have seen a journalist condemned because he had said there was no force without matter and no matter without force. It is abominable. The real conspirators are the Catholics and the Clericals. See how they are conspiring as to the Ferry bill, which will never be enforced. From the Bishop to the Beadle they are all astir. The priests' salaries must be abolished; that will be a beginning.

Do you, then, admit an atheistic State?

Why not? The law is atheistic.

No, the law protects all. It is not atheistic. It does not affirm, but it does not deny.

Well, the State should be atheistic, for I maintain that the law is so.

Would you allow believers to pay the expenses of their worship?

Yes, but not by subscriptions.

Would you leave the churches open?

Yes, but watch the preaching.

But what substitute would you find for worship?

Voltaire has already answered, "I rid them of a monster and they ask me what I shall put in its place."

But your measures against Catholicism are not enough to form a programme.

You are always thinking of a programme. I have no programme. A thing is bad, I substitute something else, to see to the application of it. Taxation is bad, it must be modified. He who works must be relieved, he who possesses, taxed; [with] salaries being at the same time augmented, and then you restore the equilibrium.

But then you destroy property.

No; I chiefly tax capital, and I forbid the reconstruction of large properties. There must at the same time be perfect freedom of the press and public meetings to discuss all the reforms.

That is to say, you would cover France with a network of tyrannical clubs, which would destroy liberty, and with a press which would advocate utopias.

It is always with these phrases that concessions are refused to the spirit of the revolution which is the spirit of modern times.

Do you share the theories of those who desire the abolition of standing armies, the community of goods, and all those monstrous doctrines which will not bear examination?

I think the expenditure must be reduced and pensions abolished, and armies are a cause of crime and a menace to liberty.

Yes, but would you advise France to disarm in existing circumstances?

No; but she must be armed differently.

Do you believe in a nation armed and responding to the appeal of the country?

No; the Army must not be a mob, but France must be armed differently.

Would you abolish titles?

I think it is ridiculous to style a Minister "His Excellency."

Are you shocked at the word "Monsieur," also?

No, that is immaterial. I remember that in 1848 *Charivari* had a caricature of two men, one of whom said to the other, "Monsieur, je vous défends de m'appeler citoyen," while the other replied, "Citoyen, je vous défends de m'appeler Monsieur." But it is immaterial to me, citoyen or Monsieur.

If you go out, will you speak much in public?

Yes, if there are clubs, otherwise I do not care about it.

Have you often spoken in public?

Yes; during the siege I was much listened to.

Do you write much?

No; in prison a manuscript is never your own.

Do you think the Chamber will confirm your election?

I know nothing about it. Individually the Chamber perhaps has intelligence, but as a whole it is very poor, and so was the National Assembly.

I do not agree with you. The Assembly contained superior men—Thiers, Louis Blanc, De Broglie, Buffet, Jules Simon—

He stopped me ironically.

You call Jules Simon an intelligent man; a man who ascends the tribune to submit a programme, and in a country where the press, the electors, the elected, the entire nation, is divided into Republicans and Conservatives, says, amid the applause of that Assembly, "I am profoundly Republican, but profoundly a Conservative." That ought to destroy a man, it is so ridiculous.

He meant that he was not a revolutionary.

That is what I reproached him with.

You will soon be released.

I do not think so; they are too anxious to keep me.

No, I think you will leave, but not before the 3rd of June.

Ah, they want to prevent my being a Deputy.

Well, you want to prevent them from governing; it is very natural they should not make you eligible;

but after the 3rd of June I believe you will be liberated.

Who knows if even then they will let me go? But they are wrong not to amnesty everybody, for the thing will always have to be begun over again.

If you were Deputy, what would you do? You would propose the unlimited amnesty, separation of Church and State, the freedom of the Commune or federation; you would have nobody with you in the Chamber.

There are very few indeed; but by degrees all that would change, the electors would return a revolutionary majority, and then—

I changed the conversation. He spoke of his health, of the heart disease, which obliged him to live only on fruits, vegetables, milk, and eggs. He seemed at bottom to distrust the food given him—the mania of old prisoners. I rose feeling ill at ease beside this obstinate mind full of dreams of demolition, and with only negative theories of reconstitution. As he knew, moreover, I should publish what he said, he probably did not say to what length he would push the work of destruction. On my rising to leave, he had a passing gleam of French gaiety.

I do not offer to see you to the gate, he said.

He really has the option, though he does not use it, of walking in the court. I knocked for the door to be opened.

Then you have seen all the remarkable men of the time.

Well, I have seen many.

And you are going to publish your visit?

Yes, and I will send it to you.

I accept your offer, for I read English; and what interested me most in England was the outdoor stump-orators. In France they would be put in prison.

Because in France they would preach the overthrow of the Government. What can I do for you?

Tell them to give me another lamp—this exasperates me.

You do not need me for that; the governor will give you all you want.

But I prefer not to ask for it.

The door opened, he wished me a good journey, and we parted.

# Endnotes

1 "Libérer l'Enfermé," *Instructions pour une prise d'armes; L'éternité par les astres*, eds Miguel Abensour & Valentin Pelosse (2000: 21). Herafter Abensour & Pelosse.

2 On Blanqui's moral naturalism, see Frank Chouraqui, "Liberté, Imaginaire et Ordre Révolutionnaire" in Lisa Block de Behar (ed.), *Blanqui: léternité par les Astres* (Geneva and Paris: Honoré Champion, 2018) 47–57.

3 See Borde, Guth, Vilenkin (2003).

4 Laplace (1814: 95–6).

5 Kahane (2008: 16).

6 Abensour & Pelosse 189.

7 Blanqui, "Toast of February 25, 1851," in Blanqui (1971: 101).

8 Nietzsche (2005). Hereafter *Zarathustra*.

9 Lichtenberger (1899: 204). See also, Batault (1904), Fouillée (1901), and Miller (1903).

10 Fouillée (1909).

11 D'Iorio (2011).

12 Mencken (1913: 117).

13 The translation, by Keith Ansell-Pearson (2006: 231), appears in his "The Incorporation of Truth: Towards the Overhuman."

14 Andreas-Salomé (2001: 131). Hereafter Andreas-Salomé.

15 Andreas-Salomé 131.

16 NF Summer–Autumn 1884, 26[376]: KSA 11/250.

17 To his sister, January 31, 1872, quoted in Abensour & Pelosse 20.

18 Simmel (1991: 172–8).

19 It seems that the main difference between Nietzsche and Blanqui, namely the insistence of the former on infinite time over and above infinite space, and therefore his insistence on repetition, is related to his energetic rather than materialistic paradigm. In a famous *Nachlaß* entry known as the "time-atom fragment," written the year following Blanqui's *Eternity*, Nietzsche explicitly declares that a cosmology of forces involves a cosmology of time, and that time should not be divided to the infinite, but rather, that it is consituted of "time-atoms." The idea of eternal recurrence seems to be at hand. See *Nachlaß* 26[11] & [12]. It is impossible to assert with certainty that Nietzsche had any knowledge of Blanqui's writing at that point (it had just been mentioned in the second edition of Lange's *History of Materialism* of the same year), but if this should be confirmed, it is likely that many of the mysteries of the time-atom fragment, especially phrases such as "the whole world at a stroke" and "all those cosmogonies" may be given clarifications.

20 Rancière (2002: 7–26).

21 Abensour & Pelosse 402.

22 Brobjer (2008: 225).

23 Lange (1925: 151, note 73).

24 Brobjer 225, and 83 and related note 128.

25 14[123] and [133] 1888; *Beyond Good & Evil* §224, 274, KSA 11 [413]; *The Anti-Christ* §4; *The Genealogy of Morality* III §14.

26 UM: III §7.

27 For despite what is commonly accepted in the Nietzsche scholarship, there need not be a tension between Nietzsche's thought of eternal recurrence and his notion of the Übermensch; in fact, the latter is a consequence of the former. Nietzsche begins his *Nachlaß* entry thus: "My question is not to find out what shall take over from the human: but rather, what type of human must be chosen, demanded, and bred." It is existing cases—the lucky strokes—that must be called Übermenschen, and it is for culture to optimize the random and wasteful productivity of nature in order to make such lucky strokes less rare.

28 *Zarathustra*, "On Great Events."

29 Schopenhauer too, a proven read of Nietzsche's, had written of the "cold skins" of dead stars in *The World as Will and Representation* (1966: 2. 1. 3, quoted in Parkes' notes to his translation of *Zarathustra*). Schopenhauer, however, did not speak of the relationship of the cosmos to mankind or of the earth having any sort of disease, be it mankind or otherwise.

30 KSA 13, 1888, 11[72], 34. Rey (1927: 7).

31 25[7] 1884.

32 Benjamin (1999: 25). Hereafter *Arcades*.

33 Letter of January 6, 1938 to Horkheimer, in Walter Benjamin (1994).

34 *Arcades* 115.

35 Benjamin to Horkheimer, April 16, 1938. See also his letter to Horkheimer, January 6, 1938. On the connections between Blanqui's *Eternity* and Baudelaire, see *Arcades* 352–3 & 362. See also Miller (2008: 279–96).

36 See, for instance, "Theses on the Philosophy of History," especially, Thesis XII.

37 To Horkheimer, January 6, 1938.

38 See, for example, Benjamin's attempt at linking Blanqui to Baudelaire by way of some second-hand reports about one of Blanqui's co-conspirators, Raoul Rigault, whose sense of humor Benjamin believes to be reminiscent of Baudelaire's in "The Paris of the Second Empire in Baudelaire" in Benjamin (2006: 49, see also 50–2). Hereafter, *Essays on Baudelaire*.

39 *Essays on Baudelaire* 129.

40 *Arcades* 329.

41 Benjamin, "Paris, capitale du XIXè siècle" (2003).

42 Buck-Morss (1991: 53, 106).

43 *Arcades* 15.

44 *Arcades* 119.

45 Heidegger declared: "Everything is functioning. That is precisely what is awesome. That everything functions, that the functioning propels everything more and more toward further functioning, and that technicity increasingly dislodges man and uproots him from the earth. I don't know if you were shocked, but I was [certainly] shocked when a short time ago I saw the pictures of the earth taken from the moon. We do not need atomic bombs at all [to uproot us]—the uprooting of man is already here. All our relationships have become merely technical ones. It is no longer upon an earth that man lives today." Heidegger (1981: 56).

46 Block de Behar (2003: 46). Hereafter *Borges*. Among the "many others" Block de Behar is alluding to, one should count "The Aleph" in which Borges indulges in a little game around Blanqui's name. By coining the term "Blanquiceleste" as a color that describes the sky, his character Daneri, who "has his mind set on putting the entire surface [redondez] of the earth in verse," is especially proud of this new coinage which, he says, "does evoke [sugiere] the sky." ("El Aleph," Borges' emphasis, in *Borges* 1984: 620–1,

hereafter Obras completas). Interestingly, the new coinage and the associated pun (Blanqui sounds like blanco—white in Spanish) does not appear in Norman Thomas di Giovanni's translation, which was corrected by Borges himself. In the English translation, the entire passage is reworked, suggesting that its only function was to evoke Blanqui and therefore could only be achieved in Spanish. See Borges, "The Aleph" (1970).

47 Borges' reference to Le Bon should not be read as an acknowledgment of the place of the sociologist's speculations on a par with those, more creative, of Blanqui and Nietzsche. If it is true that, particularly in chapters 1 and 3, Le Bon's 1881 *L'Homme et les sociétés* presents a thesis very close to Blanqui's, a mere look at Le Bon's choices of subtitles suggests that the influence borders on plagiarism. Le Bon's tone as well as several key phrases are taken directly out of Blanqui's text, and used to no other effect. See Le Bon (1881).

48 Borges, "El tiempo circular," *Obras completas* 393.

49 Obras completas 471.

50 Borges 43.

51 The very famous passage from Pascal that Blanqui is quoting only approximately here is ambiguous and seems to refer both to god and to the world. Pascal writes: "The entire visible world is nothing but an imperceptible stroke of the pen within the wide embrace of nature. No idea is able to approach it. Try as we might inflate our conceptions above and beyond the imaginable spaces, all we bring forth are mere atoms, at the cost of the reality of things. It is an infinite sphere whose center is everywhere, the circumference nowhere. Indeed, it is the greatest sensible character of god that our imagination be stranded in this thought." Blaise Pascal, *Oeuvres complètes*

(Paris: Gallimard, Pléiade, 1954) 1105, my emphasis.

52 An allusion to Epicurus: "Of bodies, some are composite, others the elements of which these composite bodies are made. These elements are indivisible and unchangeable—necessarily so, if things are not all to be destroyed and pass into non-existence. They are strong enough to endure when composite bodies are broken up, because they possess a solid nature, and are incapable of being anywhere or anyhow dissolved. It follows that the beginning of everything must be indivisible, corporeal entities." Additionally: "As the universe is not comprehended by comparison with something outside, it has no boundary and no limit. And since it has no limit it is unlimited or infinite. Moreover, the universe is infinite both by reason of the multitude of atoms and the extent of space. For, if space were infinite and the number of bodies finite, the bodies would not have stayed around but would have been dispersed throughout infinite space, because they would not have met with anything that might support or keep them in place by coming into collision with them. Alternatively, if space were finite, there would not be room for an infinity of bodies." *Stoics & Epicureans*, tr. R.D. Hicks (New York: Charles Scribner's Sons, 1910) fragments 50 and 53. Note how Epicurus, like Blanqui, uses from the outset the doctrine of atomism to solve the problem of ontogenesis, before immediately confronting the infinity of the universe.

53 Blanqui uses modern metric leagues, equivalent to 4 Kms or 2.5 miles.

54 9.7 light-years. An 1838 experiment by F.W. Bessel (1784–1846) established that the 61st star (often called the Bessel Star) of the Cygnus (or the constellation of the Swan) was the closest of its constellation to the earth. It was the first time the distance of any

star had been calculated reliably. Bessel calculated that the star was 10.4 light years away; the figure has since been corrected to 11.4 light years.

55 Two years after the publication of *Eternity*, Swedish chemist Per Teodor Cleve (1840–1905) used spectrometry to establish that Didymium was in fact a complex mixture of two simple elements, which he called Praseodymium (Pr) and Neodymium (Nd).

56 The modern debate on the physical status of light goes back at least to Descartes, who advocated something like the emission theory of light, and Huyghens, who prefigured the wave theory. It was however revived in more technical terms after Newton's ambivalent position, expressed in his *Optics* (1704). The followers of Newton seem to have been more resolute in this view than Newton himself, and the emission theory has since been associated with Newton's name. The emission theory regarded light as made up of particles sharpened into points that allowed them to penetrate certain (transparent) surfaces and bounce off some other (opaque) surfaces. The wave theory, on the other hand, suggested that light (and sound) were only waves within the 'ether,' i.e., movements of this ether, but movements without mobiles. Although the final refutation of the emission theory is widely regarded to have been delivered by the experiments of Comstock (1910) and De Sitter (1913), we may consider Blanqui correct in asserting that the emission theory was all but moribund by the 1870s. Blanqui has in mind the work of Arago's brilliant young associate Fresnel, who finalized the wave theory and provided a host of counter arguments to the emission theory. Those were mostly based upon one untenable implication of the emissions theory, namely that any luminescent object should be regarded as somehow projecting the light particles toward the objects it revealed. "According to Newton's system, the luminescent molecules spring

forth from the radiant bodies to reach us. But isn't it likely that in a body that throws light, the molecules must be projected with more or less speed, considering that they are not all subjected to the same circumstances? Yet, if one admits that the luminescent molecules, when they leave the sun for example, may have different speeds, it follows that they might have different degrees of refractability... It would result from this that the very first rays to reach us after a solar eclipse should be the red rays. But, according to a calculation I have carried out, enough time would elapse between the arrival of the red and purple rays for us to be able to perceive the difference in color. Yet, experience shows that this is not the case... I am very tempted to believe in the vibrations, of some particular fluid, as in the way that light and heat are distributed." Fresnel, Letter of July 5, 1814 to Léonor Fresnel, quoted in Robert D'Adhemar, *La philosophie des sciences & le problème religieux* (Paris: Bloud, 1904) 18. For Fresnel, therefore, and later for Maxwell (1865) himself, the speed of light must be a constant and therefore, the differences in colors cannot be attributed to differences in the speed of the particles supporting them. Further, the differences between such speeds should, in the emission picture, always be expressed as differences in colors, which is not the case. See also Laplace, *Exposition* 361.

57 Blanqui's meaning is hard to grasp here. He does not mean to challenge the wave theory, rather, he points out that, since the debate between waves and emissions is now obsolete, our attention should focus on debates between different versions of the wave theory. In this debate, Blanqui notes that spectral analysis, or spectrometry, provides indications that luminescent stars are not electrically fueled but are really flaming objects, therefore destined to be consumed and die, and that the earth is most likely an old, cold sun. This shall allow him to assert that

worlds in fact can die and resurrect forever and that all astronomical objects are kin. Spectrometry is a method that allows one to establish the chemical nature of remote objects through an analysis of the light they produce. It was thanks to spectrometry that Cecilia Payne-Gaposchkin suggested in 1925 that the sun was composed of gases, a fact established four years later by H.N. Russell. See H.N. Russell, "On the Composition of the Sun's Atmosphere," *The Astrophysical Journal*, Vol. 70 (1929) 11–60. Blanqui's sources on spectrometry are uncertain, but Herschel's observations on the infrared light coming from the sun in 1800 may be regarded as inaugurating solar spectroscopy, followed by Joseph Fraunhoffer's invention of the spectroscope in 1814 and his subsequent spectrometric observations of the sun, revealing many features of its chemical constitution, including the preponderance of hydrogen. A possible source for Blanqui could be the 1869 issue of the *Annales de chimie et de physique* (published less than three years before Blanqui's Eternity), in which all aspects of spectral analysis and wave theory are discussed in detail, and whose extended review section presents an impressive range of new works of solar spectrometry and wave theory. See *Annales de chimie et de physique* (Paris: Masson, 1869).

58 Pierre-Simon Laplace (1749–1827), French mathematician, astronomer, philosopher and politician.

59 Friedrich Wilhelm Herschel (1738–1832), British astronomer & composer. Blanqui writes "Herschell" probably following several editions of *Laplace's Exposition* (including the 5th Brussels edition by de Vroom of 1826 and the 6th Brussels edition by Rémy of 1829, and the printing of the Exposition as part of the *Complete Works of Laplace of the Imprimerie Royale*, Paris, 1846). Laplace gives ample credit to Herschel himself in several works, including

Blanqui's source, the *Exposition*. To our knowledge, there is no reason to suppose that Blanqui had first-hand knowledge of Herschel's writings.

60 Francois Arago, *Astronomie populaire* (1st edition, 1855) Vol. 2, Book 17, Ch. 37, p. 475.

61 Laplace, *Exposition du système du monde* (6th edition, 1835). Hereafter *Exposition*, Vol. 2, pps. 140, 167. The italics are Blanqui's.

62 Ibid. 234. "Somewhere else" should not be taken to mean "in another work"; indeed, it seems Blanqui's main—and possibly only—source on Laplace is the Exposition.

63 Presumably, Laplace, *Exposition*, ibid., 294. Blanqui's quote is only very remotely reminiscent of Laplace's text here.

64 The quote seems to be an approximation of Francois Arago, *Des comètes en général, et en particulier de celles qui doivent paraître en 1832 & 1835*, 3rd Edition (Paris: Bachelier, 1834) 106. A report on the book by Francoeur provides a paraphrase of Arago's text that seems closer (although by no means identical) to Blanqui's version. See L-B Francoeur, *Uranographie ou traité elémentaire d'astronomie à l'usage des personnes peu versé-es en mathématiques*, 5th edition (Paris: Bachelier, 1837) 228.

65 See note 11 above.

66 Laplace does not use this exact phrase anywhere. The idea seems to be Blanqui's recollection of Laplace's note VII of the *Exposition*, where, following Buffon, Laplace discusses stellar groups in terms of a common origin and attributes their differences entirely to different masses and therefore to motion patterns.

67 Ten years later, Nietzsche wrote in his famous aphorism entitled "The Madman": "What were we doing when we unchained this earth from its sun? Whither

is it moving now? Whither are we moving? Away from all suns? Are we not plunging continually? Backward, sideward, forward, in all directions? Is there still any up or down? Are we not straying as through an infinite nothing? Do we not feel the breath of empty space?" Friedrich Nietzsche, *The Gay Science*, tr. Walter Kaufmann (New York: Vintage, 1974) §125.

68 This seems to be a recollection of note VII of Laplace's *Exposition*. See also note 16 above.

69 Laplace, *Exposition* 482. Along with the next quotation, which belongs to the next page of Laplace's book, this is Blanqui's only exact quotation from Laplace in *Eternity by the Stars*.

70 A twist on a famous phrase attributed to King Louis XV (1710–74), who is believed to have expressed his position as an absolute monarch with the phrase, "après moi le déluge," literally, "after me, the flood."

71 Laplace, *Exposition* 483. Blanqui made minor alterations to the original text. See note 19 above.

72 Approximate quotation from the *Exposition*, 2nd edition (Paris: Duprat, 1798) 347–8. This passage does not appear in subsequent editions.

73 The supernova (SN) 1572—also called SR 10—appeared in early November 1572 within the Milky Way constellation of Cassiopeia. It was immediately reported by several observers, including the great Tycho Brahe (1546—1601), who developed his findings in his *De nova* and published them the following year.

74 SN 1604, also known as Kepler's Star, appeared in October 1604 in the Milky Way constellation of Ophiuchus. It was most systematically observed by Johannes Kepler (1571–1630), who presented his findings the same year in his *De stella nova*. Kepler

was a student of Tycho and one of the greatest and most intriguing minds of the scientific Renaissance.

75 The Menaechmi, a comic play by the Roman playwright Plautus (*c.* 254–184 BC), is based on the mistaken identities of two twin brothers. Blanqui seems to be extending the metaphor of the blood relatedness of all celestial bodies: it seems any world can pass as the other and be accepted in each other's home as master of the house interchangeably (see especially Act II, scenes 2 and 3).

76 Georges-Eugène, Baron d'Haussmann (1809–1891) was a civic planner and Prefect of the Seine department. He oversaw the rebuilding of large sections of Paris between 1853 and 1870. He worked closely with Napoleon III in a restructuring of the city, which Blanqui regarded as an attempt to prevent urban insurrections. Blanqui's swipe at Haussmann's "work of destruction" was noted by Walter Benjamin in his *Arcades Project* (1999) 25, 145, passim.

77 Emanuel, Marquis de Grouchy (1766–1847) was one of Napoleon's most prominent generals. His greatest victory was over the Prussians at the Battle of Wavre of June 14–15, 1815. This was an ironic victory that took place almost exactly at the same time as Napoleon's final defeat at the hands of the British, allied to the Prussians, at Waterloo (June 18, 1815). Grouchy's "mistake"—his engagement at Wavre, which left Napoleon's right wing undefended—is a canonical example of the ironies of history that Blanqui's hypothesis contributes to explain. The host of forthcoming examples of narrow military victories and defeats provided by Blanqui are only meant to emphasize how his hypothesis gives a new coloring to our sense of historical irony.

78 The Battle of Marengo (June 14, 1800), in the Piedmont region of Italy, was a narrow but brilliant victory of Napoleon's forces over the Austrians. The

resounding success and glory for Napoleon is widely believed to have consolidated his position following his accession to power in November 1799.

79 The Battle of Valmy (September 20, 1792), in the North Eastern French region of Champagne-Ardennes, was a surprise and decisive victory of the French revolutionary army of volunteers over the Prussian forces intent on crushing the new Republic and re-establishing the French monarchy.

80 The Battle of Sadowa, also called Battle of Königgrätz, was the final victory of Prussia over Austria in the Austro-Prussian war. At the time of writing, the memory of the Austrian's narrow defeat under general Ludwig von Benedek (1804–81) was probably still fresh in Blanqui's mind, and in his readers'. The disastrous defeat was widely blamed on Benedek's failing to seize the oportunity afforded him by the Prussian forces that had momentarily separated into two. Benedek did not engage the two sections separately and went on to lose the battle.

81 The Battle of Pharsalus (central Greece) took place in the summer of 48 BC. It was another military turning point in which the overwhelming forces of Pompey the Great (106 BC–48 BC) were surprisingly defeated by Julius Caesar's (100 BC–44 BC) own forces. It was the final word of the so-called Caesar's Civil War and the end of the Roman Republic. Pompey went on to seek refuge under the protection of the very young King Ptolemy XIIIth of Egypt (62/61 BC–47 BC). He was murdered upon arrival as part of a plot involving Ptolemy's close circles. Famously, Caesar would go on to be stabbed to death by a conspiracy of senators on the senate floor in 44 BC. Leibniz uses the same reference in a similar context. In the famous Proposition XIII of his Discourse on Metaphysics, he writes: "Since Julius Caesar will become perpetual Dictator and master of

the Republic and will overthrow the liberty of Rome, this action is contained in his concept, for we have supposed that it is the nature of such a perfect concept of a subject to involve everything, in fact so that the predicate may be included in the subject ut possit inesse subjecto. We may say that it is not in virtue of this concept or idea that he is obliged to perform this action, since it pertains to him only because God knows everything. But it will be insisted in reply that his nature or form responds to this concept, and since God imposes upon him this personality, he is compelled henceforth to live up to it. I could reply by instancing the similar case of the future contingencies which as yet have no reality save in the understanding and will of God, and which, because God has given them in advance this form, must needs correspond to it. But I prefer to overcome a difficulty rather than to excuse it by instancing other difficulties, and what I am about to say will serve to clear up the one as well as the other. It is here that must be applied the distinction in the kind of relation, and I say that that which happens conformably to these decrees is assured, but that it is not therefore necessary, and if anyone did the contrary, he would do nothing impossible in itself, although it is impossible ex hypothesi that that other happen. For if anyone were capable of carrying out a complete demonstration by virtue of which he could prove this connection of the subject, which is Caesar, with the predicate, which is his successful enterprise, he would bring us to see in fact that the future dictatorship of Caesar had its basis in his concept or nature, so that one would see there a reason why he resolved to cross the Rubicon rather than to stop, and why he gained instead of losing the day at Pharsalus, and that it was reasonable and by consequence assured that this would occur, but one would not prove that it was necessary in itself, nor that the contrary implied a contradiction, almost in the same way in which it is reasonable and assured that God will always do what is best although that which is less perfect is not thereby implied." G.W. Leibniz, *Discourse on Metaphysics and Other Writings*, tr. Robert Latta and George Montgomery, ed. Peter Loptson (Peterborough ON & London: Broadview Press, 2012). Blanqui seems to follow the lesson of Leibniz, who identifies the possible with the actual, the "reasonable" with the "assured," and borrows the rhetorical device of the narrowly won Battle of Pharsalus to show that randomness is only an illusion resulting from the limitation of our cognitive abilities. The crucial difference with Leibniz is of course that Blanqui expands the actual to the extension of the possible (leading to a multiversal vision), whereas Leibniz restricts the possible to the actual, leading to the famous thesis that this world is the only world possible, and reducing all possible worlds to this single world. Michel Serres provides a remarkable exposition of Leibniz's combinatory of recurrence with an enlightening discussion of Leibniz's change of heart on the question of recurrence, and of his insight that repetition should always be said of linguistic, not material elements, transforming the history of the world into the story of the world. See Michel Serres, *Le système de Leibniz et ses modèles mathématiques* (Paris: Presses Universitaires de France, 1968) 224 ff. Nietzsche seems to betray a similar Leibnizian recollection in his second *Untimely Meditation*. With a possible allusion to Blanqui, he writes: "At bottom, indeed, that which was once possible could present itself as a possibility for a second time only if the Pythagoreans were right in believing that when the constellation of the heavenly bodies is repeated the same things, down to the smallest even, must also be repeated on earth: so that whenever the stars stand in a certain relation to one another, a Stoic again joins with an Epicurean to murder Caesar, and whenever they stand in another relation, Columbus will again discover America." See Nietzsche, *Untimely Meditations*, tr. R.J. Hollingdale (Cambridge: Cambridge University Press, 1997) 69–70.

82 In Greek Mythology, the Danaids (daughters of Danaus) were made to carry water to a leaky or bottomless barrel or tub as a punishment for murdering their husbands. The image is commonly used to refer to an infinite, pointless, and repetitive task.

83 The Myrmidons were a mythological people of Ancient Greece who made up the bulk of Achilles' army during the Trojan war. They were said to be the offspring of a mortal woman and of Zeus, who had seduced her in the form of an ant. Their ant-like qualities included sheepish discipline, cohesion, and industriousness in war. Blanqui uses them to crystallize the paradox of the self-importance of humans compared to their objective place in nature. They are ants that think of themselves as gods.

84 Blanqui is playing with variations on the famous saying from Ecclesiastes 1:9: "There is nothing new under the sun" (often used in its Latin form: "Nil novi sub sole"), an expression meant to encapsulate the vanity of human existence.

85 Possible reminiscence of Shakespeare's famous Prologue to *Henry V* (often known as "O for a Muse of Fire"):

> "O for a Muse of fire, that would ascend
> The brightest heaven of invention,
> A kingdom for a stage, princes to act
> And monarchs to behold the swelling scene!
> Then should the warlike Harry, like himself,
> Assume the port of Mars; and at his heels,
> Leash'd in like hounds, should famine, sword &
> fire

Crouch for employment.
But pardon, gentles all,
The flat unraised spirits that hath dared
On this unworthy scaffold to bring forth
So great an object: can this cockpit hold
The vasty fields of France? or may we cram
Within this wooden
O the very casques
That did affright the air at Agincourt?
O, pardon! since a crooked figure may
Attest in little place a million;
And let us, ciphers to this great accompt,
On your imaginary forces work.
Suppose within the girdle of these walls
Are now confined two mighty monarchies,
Whose high upreared and abutting fronts
The perilous narrow ocean parts asunder:
Piece out our imperfections with your thoughts;
Into a thousand parts divide one man,
And make imaginary puissance;
Think when we talk of horses, that you see them
Printing their proud hoofs i'th' receiving earth;
For 'tis your thoughts that now must deck our kings,
Carry them here and there; jumping o'er times,
Turning th'accomplishment of many years
Into an hourglass: for the which supply,
Admit me
Chorus to this history;
Who prologue-like your humble patience pray,
Gently to hear, kindly to judge, our play."

William Shakespeare, *Henry V*, I.Prologue

Note the resonances between Blanqui's conspicuous metaphor of the hourglass and his "tragedy on the narrow stage" and Shakespeare's own hourglass, his "cockpit" and "the girdle of these walls," as well as the reflection of the connections between multiplication, division, imagination, writing, and the use of numbers to represent the unimaginable.

86 Probably Henri Blowitz (1825–1903), the London Times correspondent in Paris from 1873 to 1902.

# Bibliography

Robert D'Adhemar, *La philosophie des sciences et le problème religieux* (Paris: Bloud, 1904).

Lou Andreas-Salomé, *Nietzsche*, tr. & ed. by Siegfried Mandel (Urbana & Chicago: University of Illinois Press, 2001).

Keith Ansell-Pearson (ed.), *A Companion to Nietzsche* (London & New York: Blackwell, 2006).

Francois Arago, *Des comètes en général, et en particulier de celles qui doivent paraître en 1832 et 1835*, 3rd edition (Paris: Bachelier, 1834).

——*Astronomie populaire*, 1st edition, 4 vols (Paris: Gide et Baudry, 1854–57).

Georges Batault, "L'Hypothèse du retour éternel devant la science moderne," *Revue philosophique de la France & de l'étranger*, Vol. 57 (1904) 158–167.

Walter Benjamin, "Über den Begriff der Geschichte," *Gesammelten Schriften* Vol 1:2 (Frankfurt am Main: Suhrkamp Verlag, 1974).

——*Correspondence*, tr. Manfred R. Jacobson and Evelyn M. Jacobson, eds Gershom Scholem and Theodor W. Adorno (London & Chicago: University of Chicago Press, 1994).

——*The Arcades Project*, tr. Howard Eiland and Kevin McLaughlin, ed. Rolf Tiedemann (Cambridge, MA & London: Harvard University Press, 1999).

——*Écrits Francais* (Paris: Gallimard, 2003).

——*The Writer of Modern Life: Essays on Baudelaire*, tr. Howard Eiland, Edmund Jephcott, Rodney Livingston & Harry Zohn, ed. Michæl W. Jennings (Cambridge, MA & London: Harvard University Press, 2006).

Louis-Auguste Blanqui, *Textes choisis* (Paris: Les Éditions Sociales, 1971).

——*Instructions pour une prise d'armes; l'Éternité par les astres*, eds Miguel Abensour & Valentin Pelosse (Paris: Sens et Tonka, 2000).

——*L'Éternité par les astres* (Paris: Les Impressions Nouvelles, 2002).

——*The Blanqui Reader: Political Writings, 1830–1880*, ed. by Philippe le Goff and Peter Hallward (London: Verso, 2018).

Lisa Block de Behar, *Borges: The Passion of an Endless Quotation*, tr. William Egginton (Albany: State University of New York Press, 2003).

——*L'Éternité par les Astres d'Auguste Blanqui*, ed. Lisa Block de Behar (Paris and Geneva: Honoré Champion, 2019).

Gustave Le Bon, *L'homme et les sociétés, leurs origines et leur histoire.* First part: "L'homme: Développement physique et intellectuel" (Paris: Rothschild, 1881).

Arvind Borde, Alan H. Guth, and Alexander Vilenkin, "Inflationary Spacetimes are not Past-Complete," *Physical Review Letters* (2003) 1–4.

Jorge Luis Borges: *Obras completas* 1923–1972 (Buenos Aires: Emecé Editores, 1984).

——"The Aleph," *The Aleph and Other Stories, 1933–1969*, tr. Norman Thomas di Giovanni (revised by the author) (London: E.P. Dutton, 1970).

Thomas H. Brobjer, *Nietzsche's Philosophical Context: An Intellectual Biography* (Urbana & Chicago: University of Illinois Press, 2008).

Susan Buck-Morss, *The Dialectics of Seeing: Walter Benjamin and the Arcades Project* (Cambridge, MA & London: The MIT Press, 1991).

Frank Chouraqui, "Liberté Imaginaire et Ordre Révolutionnaire," in Lisa Block de Behar, ed., *L'Éternité par les Astres d'Auguste Blanqui* (Paris and Geneva: Honoré Champion, 2019) 47–57.

Collective, *Annales de chimie et de physique* (Paris: Masson, 1869).

Alfred Fouillée, "La morale aristocratique du surhomme," *Revue des deux mondes*, Vol. 71, Issue 5 (1901) 81–112.

——"Note sur Nietzsche et Lange, 'le retour éternel'," *Revue philosophique de la France et de l'étranger*, Vol. 67 (1909) 519–525.

Louis-Benjamin Francoeur, *Uranographie ou traité élémentaire d'astronomie à l'usage des personnes peu verséees en mathématiques*, 5th edition (Paris: Bachelier, 1837).

Peter Hallward, "Blanqui's Bifurcations," *Radical Philosophy* 185 (May–June 2014) 36–44.

——*Blanqui & Political Will* (London: Verso, Forthcoming).

Martin Heidegger, "Only a God Can Save Us," The *Spiegel* Interview (1966), tr. William J. Richardson, in

*Heidegger: The Man and the Thinker*, ed. Thomas Sheehan (Chicago: Precedent Publishing, 1981) 45–69.

Robert Drew Hicks (ed. & tr.), *Stoics and Epicureans* (New York: Charles Scribner's Sons, 1910).

Paolo D'Iorio, "The Eternal Return: Genesis & Interpretation," tr. Frank Chouraqui, *The Agonist*, Vol. 4, Issue 1 (spring 2011) 1–43.

Jean-Pierre Kahane, "Hasard et déterminisme chez Laplace," *Les cahiers rationalistes*, 593 (March–April 2008) 1–16.

Friedrich Albert Lange, *The History of Materialism*, tr. Ernest Chester Thomas (London: Kegan Paul, Trench, Trübner & Co., 1925).

Pierre-Simon de Laplace, *Exposition du système du monde*

2nd Paris edition (Paris: Duprat, 1798).

5th Brussels edition (Brussels: de Vroom, 1826).

6th Brussels edition (Brussels: Rémy, 1829).

6th Paris edition (Paris: Bachelier, 1835).

——*Essai philosophique sur les probabilités* (Paris: Courcier, 1814).

——*Oeuvres complètes de Laplace* (Paris: Imprimerie Royale, 1846).

Gottfried Wilhelm Leibniz, *Discourse on Metaphysics and Other Writings*, tr. Robert Latta and George Montgomery, ed. Peter Loptson (Peterborough, ON & London: Broadview Press, 2012).

Henri Lichtenberger, *Die Philosophie Friedrich Nietzsches: übersetzt und mit einer Einleitung versehen*, tr. Elisabeth Förster-Nietzsche (Dresden & Leipzig: Carl Reigner Verlag, 1899).

Henry Louis Mencken, *The Philosophy of Friedrich Nietzsche* (Boston: Luce & Co., 1913).

Charles Ransom Miller, "Friedrich Nietzsche, his Philosophy of Social Life, of Morals, and of Human Progress Toward a Higher Ideal State," *New York Times Saturday Review of Books* (March 7, 1903).

Tyrus Miller, "Eternity No More: Walter Benjamin on Eternal Recurrence," *Given World and Time, Temporalities in Context*, ed. Tyrus Miller (Budapest: The Central European University Press, 2008) 279–296.

Friedrich Nietzsche, *Kritische Gesamtausgabe*, eds Giorgio Colli and Mazzino Montinari (Berlin & New York: Walter de Gruyter, 1967 ff.).

——*The Antichrist* in *The Portable Nietzsche*, tr. & ed. Walter Kaufmann (London: Penguin, 1982) 565–656.

——*Beyond Good and Evil*, tr. Marion Faber (Oxford: Oxford University Press, 1998).

——*The Gay Science*, tr. Walter Kaufmann (New York: Vintage, 1974).

——*On the Genealogy of Morality*, ed. Keith Ansell-Pearson, tr. Carol Diethe (Cambridge: Cambridge University Press, 1994).

——*Untimely Meditations*, tr. R.J. Hollingdale (Cambridge: Cambridge University Press, 1997).

——*Thus Spoke Zarathustra*, tr. Graham Parkes (Oxford & New York: Oxford University Press, 2005).

Blaise Pascal, *Oeuvres complètes* (Paris: Gallimard, Pléiade, 1954).

Jacques Rancière, "Préface," Auguste Blanqui, *L'éternité par les astres* (Paris: Les Impressions Nouvelles, 2002).

Abel Rey, *Le retour éternel et la philosophie de la physique* (Paris: Flammarion, 1927).

Henry Norris Russell, "On the Composition of the Sun's Atmosphere," *The Astrophysical Journal*, Vol. 70 (1929) 11–60.

Arthur Schopenhauer, *The World as Will and Representation*, tr. by E.F.J. Payne (New York: Dover, 1966).

Michel Serres, *Le système de Leibniz et ses modèles mathématiques* (Paris: Presses Universitaires de France, 1968).

William Shakespeare, *The Works of William Shakespeare* (London & New York: Frederick Warne & Co., 1890).

Georg Simmel, *Schopenhauer & Nietzsche*, tr. Helmut Loiskandl, Deena Weinstein, Michael Weinstein (Urbana & Chicago: University of Illinois Press, 1991).